Creating an Intentional Ministry

Creating an Intentional Ministry

Edited by
John E. Biersdorf

Abingdon   Nashville

CREATING AN INTENTIONAL MINISTRY
Copyright © 1976 by Abingdon

Library of Congress Cataloging in Publication Data

Main entry under title:

Creating an intentional ministry.

  Bibliography: p.
  Includes index.
  1. Pastoral theology—Addresses, essays, lectures. I. Biersdorf, John E., 1930-
BV4011.C68   253'.2   75-40463

ISBN 0-687-09810-6

Scripture quotations noted RSV are from the Revised Standard Version of the Bible, copyrighted 1946, 1952, and 1971, by the Division of Christian Education, National Council of Churches, and are used by permission.

The chapter entitled "Getting a Job" is based on John C. Harris' "The Minister Looks for a Job," published by the Alban Institute, Inc., Washington, D.C., in 1974, and is used by permission of the publisher.

Material from *The Seminarian's Vocational Planning Handbook* by Thomas E. Brown is reprinted by permission of the Center for Professional Development in Ministry and the author.

Material from "First Steps" by Thomas E. Brown is reprinted from *The Christian Ministry* (May, 1974) by permission of *The Christian Ministry,* Christian Century Foundation, Chicago, Ill.

MANUFACTURED BY THE PARTHENON PRESS AT
NASHVILLE, TENNESSEE, UNITED STATES OF AMERICA

To those ministers who by their commitment and effectiveness have taught us about intentionality and negotiation

CONTENTS

INTRODUCTION

The intentional minister. The book is dedicated to him or her—to bringing about a fuller understanding of the particular challenges and opportunities facing the clergy in mid-career in the mid-seventies, and to identifying resources for more effectively dealing with those realities. We are advocates in this volume—advocates of a style of ministry that we believe to be distinctively faithful and effective, and of the application of that style to the specifics of the day-by-day professional and personal work and life of the minister. The authors represented here have an almost awesome intimate knowledge of the stuff of ministry, as they have known it in their own lives, as they have been involved in the pain and joy of other ministers, and as they have attempted to address the issues of ministry in their various specialized professional roles. Therefore, we are advocates in this volume, believing strongly that some things ought to be done to alleviate the difficulties and to increase the opportunities for service and fulfillment in ministry. There is even some dialogue and conflict between the various viewpoints in this book, since the issues are not simple and convictions often differ about the best way to resolve them. We are also reporters of research. Amid all the mix of personal opinion, exhortation, and research which has been published, we have tried to identify those empirical studies carried out with credible social scientific methodology, and to test our advocacies against them. We were concerned that our convictions should not only be based on human experience, but, where possible, should be broadly and factually supported by the experience of many others. One of our chief frustrations was to discover how many areas have few or no relevant and carefully done empirical studies. In fact, we hope that one of the benefits of the book may be to stimulate research in some of those areas.

Contemporary understanding of ministry has been influenced by the crucible of social activism in the 1960s, and the social apathy and conservatism of the mid-seventies. Ministers out of seminary a few years have known bewildering changes in theological fashion from celebrating secularism and the death of God to the promiscuous return of religion in almost every conceivable form. But underneath the return of religion ministers often face steady institutional decline in their local churches and denominations. Most ministers can hardly have avoided the impact of new management methodologies, organizational development, and the various influences of social sciences. The long-term effect of this rationalization, secularization, and professionalization of the professional ministry is really not known. For some ministers it has made a truly effective and satisfying ministry possible for the first time. For others it has raised doubts as to how the theological doctrines of call and grace fit into the new language of goal-setting and performance evaluation. We have found an evocative image or model of ministry that we believe to be especially helpful in steering through all these external and internal shaping forces in contemporary ministry. We named it, or it named itself, by the phrase "negotiating an intentional ministry." The volume intends to be an explanation, an advocacy, of this style of ministry, and an application of it to the specific realities of professional life and work.

The first part of the book explains the model, and the chapter by Thomas Campbell, a sociologist of religion and the academic vice-president of United Theological Seminary in New Brighton, Minnesota, describes sociologically the arenas of negotiation within which the intentional minister works. The model is then applied to the minister's career in Part II. Out of his extensive research and clinical experience in founding and directing the Northeast Career Center, and the career counseling facilities at Lancaster Theological Seminary, Thomas Brown gives a highly useful and comprehensive guide to career and occupational planning. John Harris, assistant to the bishop for clergy development of the Episcopal Diocese of Washington, relates that framework to the specifics of getting a job. Connolly Gamble, the founding and continuing executive secretary of the Society for the Advancement of Continuing Education for Ministry and the director of continuing education at Union Theological Seminary in Richmond, Virginia, advocates a lifelong process of continuing education as a necessary implementation of intentional career planning.

In Part III, James Gunn, executive director of Professional Church Leadership for the National Council of Churches, and G. Douglass Lewis, coordinator of Parish Development for the Hartford Seminary Foundation, apply the model to goal-setting, evaluation, and organizational development in the congregation. Robert Kemper, editor of *Christian Ministry* magazine and pastor of the United Church of Christ in Western Springs, Illinois, in Part IV takes ministers to task around some "small issues" that amount to massive revelation about faithfulness and effectiveness in the profession.

Part V addresses three critical social issues in negotiating an intentional ministry. Cornish Rogers, associate editor of *Christian Century* and pastor of St.

Paul's United Methodist Church in Oxnard, California, writes on the black ministry. Burnice Fjellman, associate executive of Professional Church Leadership for the National Council of Churches, discusses the problems of women in ministry. Speed Leas, director of training for the Institute for Advanced Pastoral Studies in Bloomfield Hills, Michigan, describes social change strategies that make sense for the 1970s. Stephen Mott, assistant professor of Christianity and urban society at Gordon-Conwell Theological Seminary, concludes the volume with a theological understanding of negotiation and intentionality in ministry.

I want particularly to thank Andrew Hobart, president of Minister's Life and Casualty Union, whose patient and persevering counsel made the book a reality, and the Minister's Life and Casualty Union for the grant which made the project possible. Edgar W. Mills, now assistant professor of sociology at St. John's University in Jamaica, Long Island, was the first director of the project. He originated the idea of the intentional minister, supervised the review of research, and wrote part of the first chapter. Dana Flint, a doctoral student at Temple University, acted as administrative assistant for the project and for the committee of authors. The authors worked together as a committee, shaping the model and guiding the project through its various stages, producing a book that is more the expression of community than a collection of essays. Celia Hahn, writer and editor, focused the collection of essays into a coherent whole and edited the manuscript. To these and many more, especially the many ministers who shared life with the authors and generated the need for the book, and the insights therein, our thanks, and our hope that this volume will be a helpful contribution to ministry in our time.

JOHN E. BIERSDORF

PART I

NEGOTIATING AN INTENTIONAL MINISTRY

We believe effectiveness and faithfulness in ministry result from negotiating an intentional ministry. Negotiation refers to the quality of relationships and transactions by which ministry is carried out. Intentionality refers to the style of faith and proactive behavior that is at the heart of effective ministry. The first chapter in this part introduces the model of negotiating an intentional ministry. The second chapter analyzes the complex network of persons and groups in which effective ministry is negotiated.

A New Model of Ministry

JOHN E. BIERSDORF

Out of our human experience in ministry, our analysis of research in the field, and our discussions together, an organizing principle, or model, or image of ministry evolved: *negotiating an intentional ministry.* It is an evocative image which seems especially to lift up the patterns of forces—the obstacles and opportunities—operating in the contemporary life and work of ministry. It is an organizing principle which is the most general way of summing up the implications and findings of recent research in the field, especially recent studies of stress in ministry, and the reported clinical experience of career counseling centers for clergy. And it is the basis for a verbal model of ministry, which can become a fundamental vocational self-image for understanding oneself as a professional person, organizing one's work, and evaluating one's own effectiveness. Samuel Blizzard called such a model an integrative role, which provides the goal orientation or frame of reference that governs professional relations with persons and groups.[1] Given the great diversity of possible professional activities in

John E. Biersdorf is director of the Institute for Advanced Pastoral Studies, Bloomfield Hills, Michigan.

The content of this article reflects the model of ministry developed by the working party which planned and wrote the book. Portions of the chapter were written by Edgar Mills, James Gunn, and Thomas Campbell, as well as by John Biersdorf.

ministry, and the changing and fluctuating cultural and organizational forces that influence those activities, the minister, to be effective and faithful, must consciously choose and act out an integrating role or vocational image in order to give coherence and direction to his or her professional work. We suggest that negotiating an intentional ministry is such a role or model, particularly suited to the needs and challenges of the contemporary situation. The book attempts to flesh out the model by applying it to those issues on which intentionality and negotiation are especially critical and helpful ways of understanding and grappling with the dimensions of modern ministry. Here we want to describe briefly the model itself.

NEGOTIATION

Each of the words in the model is important. "Negotiation" refers to the quality of transactions between the minister and the persons and groups with whom he or she carries out his or her professional work. Ministry as negotiation takes its shape from what Winthrop Hudson calls one of the fundamental characteristics of American religious life, namely, its voluntarism. In contrast to the settled, government-supported parishes of the Old World, in our culture, "a new beginning had to be made by individuals recruiting their own congregations out of a population which was largely unchurched."[2] American churches and synagogues have been from the beginning, and continue to be, voluntary associations—democratic in nature even when official doctrine holds otherwise, forced to adapt to cultural, social, and economic influences, and to hold laity in high importance as they continually renegotiate their existence on the basis of the felt importance of the services they offer. "Negotiation" seems to be the most powerful word to sum up the professional life-style and work of the minister who serves the church as a voluntary organization.

James Gustafson argues persuasively that the politician offers an instructive parallel to the minister as negotiator in the setting of a voluntary church. Such an interpretation can be misunderstood if one thinks of politicians who seem interested only in manipulating the needs and interests of the electorate for personal power and survival in office. It may be more appropriate to speak of the statesman, rather than the politician, for the term "statesman" connotes a person with important ethical principles or, to anticipate our argument, with intentionality. Gustafson, using the image of the politician for understanding the contemporary role of parish clergy, points out that ministers in the American context cannot assume that they will have a following. They must manifest a nearly constant concern for "building a constituency." In building that constituency they will make appeals to the values of the Christian tradition which they believe will be affirmed by the members who join the community of believers. In addition, the political leader recognizes the diversity of viewpoints within the constituency and seeks to "form a consensus." The diverse members of the constituency would each allocate resources in different ways to achieve some of the diverse goals they have in mind for the group. The political leader takes into account this diversity of interest and resource allocation in his attempts to build consensus. The formation of consensus is also related to the "diversity of gifts" which is present within the constituency. This diversity must be coordinated by the leader so that the group has "integration."

All three categories of political leadership could be fulfilled by a self-serving leader. He could well develop his constituency, form a consensus, and take account of the diversity of gifts, all for his own ends. He would be a politician in the most negative sense of that term. He becomes a statesman only when he also has "integrity and a sense of office." Max Weber, in his essay "Politics as a Vocation,"[3] begins by stressing the quality of "passion" (in the sense of devotion to a cause) as the first quality of a person who sees politics as his vocation. Without that sense of devotion to a cause, the politician has no *calling* to politics. Weber lists two other qualities of the politician, a feeling of responsibility and a sense of proportion, but neither of these qualities has any meaning without the passion which shapes the politician's vocation. To anticipate our later argument, a minister, like a politician, expresses intentionality as well as negotiation in his professional work.

The minister as negotiator, then, like the politician, must build a constituency, build consensus, and integrate the life and work of the voluntary association of the church he or she serves. In fact, ministry is a continuing process of negotiation with a variety of significant social systems, such as congregation, family, peers, denomination, seminary, neighborhood, community, and culture. Out of these negotiations (many of them quite unconscious) emerge the realities of our ministry, its shape and focus, its impact and effectiveness, its victories and defeats, its style and flavor, and its public and private significance. We negotiate our identity, our professional space, our work, our specializations, our relationships, the expectations people have of us, our study leaves, our salary and other rewards, our organizational and geographical location, and our pattern of development and growth. Our career in ministry is the story we tell (past) and the scenario we project (future) about all these negotiations with our environment and those of its special publics that constitute our personal reference groups.

These negotiations may be conscious or unconscious, planned or happenstance, satisfying or frustrating, effective or ineffective, informed by a vision or aimless. If politics in its best sense is the art of the possible, negotiation is the way in which we work together to make the possible become a reality. It involves having both vision that gives our career intentionality, and effectiveness in realizing that intention. It requires a style that is open and that trusts the partners in the negotiations to make their unique contributions to the realities that will emerge out of the negotiations. It means identifying the issues that are important and meaningful for the church and developing a consensus about the most effective strategies for addressing those issues.

Negotiation as an organizing principle for ministry is an explicitly dynamic image. All too often the organizational life of the church is approached with static images that focus in one way or another on the status of the minister. In such an approach one's identity as a minister is given rather than worked out in a day-to-day life in the community. And ministers are not inclined to negotiate, since to do so might imply a questioning of their God-given authority. In terms of conflict management theory this means always operating from a "win-lose" position with an implicit message that we do not trust anyone except ourselves, and clergy experience a "we-they" struggle which is more like warfare than the fellowship of the reconciled in the world. Understanding ministry from the perspective of negotiation presupposes that the reality of the Christian community is in some significant sense a social creation or construction and that the minister has a valuable contribution to make to that continuing creation. In every social group there is an ongoing conversation about what is happening, what it means, and what constitutes an appropriate response. Out of that conversation emerge shared values and meanings, common tasks, and shared experiences. Out of this experience, too, comes the feeling of having companions and being a trusted companion in a company of persons who share a common vision of reality and who test that vision in corporate action. The facilitating role ministers play in this ongoing conversation, the contribution we make to the conversation (perhaps it is theological expertise?), and the roles we play in the corporate action are constantly being negotiated with our companions as we go about our ministry. Out of these negotiations emerge the realities of who we are as a people and what we are about as the church.

The concept of negotiation also offers an alternative to a simplistic and usually frustrating view of one's professional career. Whatever career scenario we projected for ourselves as we began our ministry was probably based on a confidence in the ability of the system to recognize our skills and to move us through a series of pastorates to some situation that we could rightfully consider a career apex. It was not long before we began to suspect (probably about the third year in our first parish) that the system was not all that reliable. Some dropped out and others learned to live with a lot of frustration while developing some coping styles aimed primarily at influencing the relocation system. Sometimes our behavior was so oriented to setting up and getting ready for that next move that we were not really able to be present to what was happening in the here and now. When the next move didn't materialize, there were few useful behaviors at our disposal with which to deal with anger and frustration.

While not underplaying the value of a new situation in

which to negotiate new expectations for our ministry, the concept of negotiation emphasizes the importance, even the necessity, of continually working out a fresh sense of self-worth and new role expectations with our congregation and community right where we are—not simply on those infrequent occasions when we are in conversation with a pulpit nominating committee. We are seduced too easily and too quickly by a dossier-résumé system that lists the congregations or agencies we have served rather than those moments when we successfully negotiated a deeper sense of personal identity or a new role expectation with our congregation. Our career in ministry is not a disconnected series of fields of service held together by a denominational pension plan. It is a living, continuing process of interaction with others to translate vision into reality. Theologically speaking we are called to be co-creators with God in the continuing work of creation and renewal.

Negotiation requires an open style. This means a willingness to legitimate human conflict as a potentially creative force and to operate with some common ground rules about how conflict is faced and utilized. One of the resources currently available to ministers and congregations is skill training in the management and creative use of conflict. This open style also involves letting others know what you are thinking and feeling, what your values are, and what your vision is. Here again there are numerous training resources available in the areas of value clarification and communication skill training which ministers and congregations are utilizing as they move toward a more open style of church life.

The negotiation process also requires that the minister have some personal clarity about his skills, competencies, preferences, and goals. Our hunch is that congregations respond more affirmatively to ministers who have this kind of clarity than to ministers who try to do everything because of their confusion about what they can do well and what they want to do. We cannot be all things to all people at all times.

Finally, the concept of ministry as a negotiation process requires regular opportunities for ministers and congregations to talk about what is going on, to give and receive feedback on behaviors related to mission and ministry goals, and to negotiate new goals and expectations. In the last few years church organizational development has emerged as a useful tool for helping congregations to "get their game together" and for identifying the specific role expectations of the minister in facilitating the congregation's mission and ministry. A minister can do a great deal to clarify and to set new role expectations for himself or herself as he or she negotiates with a pulpit nominating committee seeking a new pastor, but in that situation there is no real opportunity for live feedback on his or her past performance as the facilitator of the congregation's work. For the negotiation process to be effective in producing a common vision and realistic expectations there need to be periodic occasions for reflection in the midst of the ongoing relationship between pastor and congregation. Family, peers, denomination, community, and society at large provide other arenas in which our career is constantly being negotiated and in which we have negotiating partners who have much at stake in how effectively we carry out our side of the negotiations and how well we facilitate the whole process.

INTENTIONALITY

It was not possible to discuss negotiation without implying the necessity of the opposite pole, intentionality, in our model of ministry. Like yin and yang in Chinese philosophy, neither negotiation nor intentionality can exist without or apart from the other in an effective and faithful ministry. The need for intentionality in ministry is shown by such findings as the fact that in 1969 58 percent of Protestant clergy expressed the feeling that the work of the church seemed futile or ineffectual; this feeling was reported as a serious problem for one-third of these, drawn from a national sample of 4,665 Protestant clergy.[4]

By the next year 30 percent of a national sample of 1,774 Roman Catholic clergy reported serious frustration in their work, and 12 percent regarded as a serious problem their conviction that they could do more outside than inside the organized church.[5]

These widespread feelings of futility, frustration, and impotence are not unique to the ministry. In fact, most people know the experience of having their daily lives determined more by pressures from their environments than by their own purposes. For some, the awareness of being bound by external circumstances and internal limits is an occasional frustration, while for others it is a daily grinding reality.

By contrast, some people do seem more in control of their world, setting goals and achieving them, maintaining directions in spite of barriers. Many of these are *intentional* people. Their experience confirms that, although environmental pressures have to be taken into account, people's own intentionality can, to a large degree, determine the direction and fruitfulness of their lives.

Consider the experience of the pastor who, when asked whether he set goals and priorities in his ministry, replied:

> From the very beginning of my ministry I have felt a consistent thrust toward teaching and interpretation. Oh, it varies from year to year, of course, and it takes many forms, but it has grown much deeper in this second

23

decade, as though one of the branches of a tree gradually enlarged and has become the central trunk. Practically all my projects and goals now have to do with interpreting the gospel, the contemporary scene, and various kinds, of people to one another. I give priorities in my work time largely on this basis.

This man's ministry is intentional, both in the everyday sense of holding conscious intentions by which he sets daily priorities among clamoring tasks, and also in the deeper sense of having an underlying direction to his work, giving it continuity and vision over the years. His intentionality is his bulwark against feelings of futility, frustration, and powerlessness in the ministry.

Intentionality has meaning at three different levels for ministers, most of whom will recognize themselves in one or more of these levels. I will discuss all three briefly and will then conclude with a listing of basic concerns of the intentional minister.

1. *Intentions.* The most obvious meaning of "intentionality" is that one has intentions, definite plans, purposes, goals toward which energy and resources are mobilized. To some degree, everyone has intentions, many of which are never carried out. But the intentional minister makes decisions about specific goals and sets out to accomplish those that he or she regards as high priorities. The opposite of intentionality at this level is *reactivity,* responding to events and pressures rather than grasping the initiative in a *proactive* way. Intentionality thus has a future orientation: it means purposefully directing one's life as much as possible rather than simply allowing it to be determined by past and present pressures.

Ministers sometimes fall into reactive behavior without realizing it. The pressure of events and demands (both inner and outer) becomes so great that one loses all control over schedule, and priorities are abandoned with

24

scarcely a backward look. A useful diagnostic question to ask is: "What (or who) determined the kind of work I have done during the past week?" The answer suggests whether you are more intentional or more reactive in your work.

When a new pastor arrives at a church, he or she does not simply receive a role. A creative process goes on in which urgencies felt within the congregation are merged with those brought by the pastor, and a working synthesis is developed; a role is *created*. Role creation is a decision-making and negotiation process, requiring a strong sense of direction to do it well. For some ministers the resulting synthesis may reflect more the pressures of their environments than their own intentions and needs. For these persons, the role of pastor may be a peripheral appendage poorly integrated with the overall structure of their lives, and staying in the ministry may depend largely upon the stability of their environmental support system. Another diagnostic question to ask yourself is: "What is usually the outcome when my own intentions conflict with the demands of my environment?" How you handle such situations gives another clue to the degree of intentionality in your ministry.

People with *consistently* intentional or reactive styles are very rare. Most of us strike a balance between our ability to grasp the initiative and the necessity to respond to the inevitable, and we are more intentional in some aspects of our lives than in others. Sometimes this is unavoidable. For example, a group of Southern black pastors said, "We can be very intentional with our congregations, but with the white power structure in our (predominantly white) denomination we just can't do it."

Nevertheless, despite variations in degree and consistency, intentionality is a dominant fact in many ministries and could be for many more. One of the reasons is the frequent emphasis placed on planning and decision-making. One man described his discovery of an intentional style thus:

> I had to make a decision—and everyone does in a parish that has problems. Either you become a party to maintaining the status quo . . . or you decide you're going to be on the cutting edge. . . . I don't think you can do them both—either you're going to be up there where the real problems are occurring and you're trying to solve a real problem in the church, or you're just a storekeeper, and I couldn't be a storekeeper.

"Storekeeping" may not be a fair description of the work-style of low-intentionality clergy, but it puts clearly the contrast between ministry which primarily responds to urgencies in the environment, and ministry which is decisive and intentional in implementing definite plans and priorities. Another useful diagnostic question is: "Twenty years from now, what will I be very glad to have done in the ministry of those years?" From various levels of yourself you will find images and feelings of a satisfying ministry emerging to guide your intentions.

The first and most obvious level of intentionality is thus having *intentions*, involving oneself in plans, setting priorities, creating one's role, and mobilizing resources for primarily proactive rather than reactive ministry. Underlying this level are two aspects of intentionality without which mere intentions prove very shallow: vocation, and the shared consciousness that change is possible.

2. *Vocation.* A deeper level of intentionality in a minister's life is often expressed as a sense of vocation. Although its most common usage refers to a specific inner conviction that God is calling one to the Christian ministry, the larger meaning of "vocation" is a summons to participate in a purpose larger than one's own, which is shared by others. Rollo May, in an extended

discussion of intentionality, distinguishes between acts of the will (what I have called "intentions") and the underlying direction, movement, and meaning of one's life. Citing William James, May says that when one seems unable to carry out specific intentions or experiences a paralysis of the will, the way out is to immerse oneself mentally in what one wishes to become, not so much to demand a decision (that throws it back into the power struggle of the will) as to let the vision of the future and the direction in which one wishes to go take over one's mind for a time, to reorient and redirect the divided will.[6]

This recourse to the underlying direction of one's life, and to what one cares for and values most strongly, is a recalling of *vocation* as an expression of intentionality far more profound than conscious intentions. Vocation in this sense includes a wide range of wishes and fantasies of what one might become, as well as a developing core of confidence that one's life has definiteness of direction and is part of a larger movement of history and humanity. A minister's long-range goals must derive from his or her awareness of vocation or the result will be inner strain and alienation. The opposite of vocation is thus a shallow, ad hoc approach to life issues, amounting at times to a kind of opportunism in making job and career decisions. This approach is exemplified in an ex-minister's remark about his move into banking: "Now I'm delighted with settling down in an organization in which no longer do I have to carry the ball of leadership, so to speak, nor am I in the limelight of criticism. I'm getting a fairly good salary, and now I can sort of coast up the ladder and have this mother of the industry care for me." This man had many intentions but little awareness of vocation.

The traditional understanding of the vocation or call to ministry is that it is not to some vague "purpose larger than our own," but to the saving knowledge of God as revealed in Jesus Christ, and a life of professional work dedicated to his service. The will to be a Christian, and the further decision to become a professional minister in the service of Christ, are ideally understood to be life-transforming, if not life-shattering, events. In fact, the New Testament looks to the two most important events of human life—birth and death—for analogies to describe the response. "Truly, truly, I say to you, unless one is born anew, he cannot see the kingdom of God. . . . Truly, truly, I say to you, unless one is born of water and the Spirit, he cannot enter the kingdom of God. That which is born of the flesh is flesh, and that which is born of the Spirit is spirit" (John 3:3, 5-6 RSV).

Jesus uses harsh words to convey the demand that one must experience the death of the ego—the surrender of all natural securities and even the sense of self, in order to enter the Kingdom of God, either as a layperson or as a professional minister. "If any man would come after me, let him deny himself and take up his cross and follow me. For whoever would save his life will lose it; and whoever loses his life for my sake and the gospel's will save it. For what does it profit a man, to gain the whole world and forfeit his life. For what can a man give in return for his life?" (Mark 8:34-37 RSV).

Too often in the history of Christianity these words have been used to encourage self-punishment and passive obedience to ecclesiastical authority. Their true purpose is to state in uncompromising terms the ultimate seriousness of the imperative.

If the response is really like death and rebirth, then neither good deeds, nor spiritual discipline, nor profound learning by themselves or in combination can suffice to bring a man or woman across that awesome barrier. For that, only love is powerful enough, as Jesus indicated in his response to the rich young man: "And

Jesus looking upon him loved him, and said to him, 'You lack one thing; go, sell what you have, and give to the poor, and you will have treasure in heaven; and come, follow me'" (Mark 10:21).

The professional minister is still understood in the church and even in the culture as a person who has experienced these realities in the depths of his or her psyche, who out of a transformed life and behavior is able to lead and nurture others in the same experience. Urban Holmes articulates this understanding of vocation in the model of the minister as the "sacramental person," one "through whom is experienced the person of the church and of Christ."[7] The church is understood to be the primal sacrament of Christ, or the *Ursakrament.*

> It is in the *history of persons* and their lives within the chosen community Israel and in the broader community of mankind that we meet God as personal. Ultimately its supreme expression is in the *person* of Christ, his life, death and resurrection. Here we perceive the promise of the fullfillment of our personhood. As Christ's ministry was that of his person, so the ministry of the *Ursakrament,* the church, is of the person. We have seen, therefore, that the essence of Christian ministry is that individual who embodies in his person the church's vocation. That is what I have called the "sacramental person" and I have said that ministerial function derives itself from this source.[8]

This depth and certainity of vocation was probably always more of an ideal than a typical reality. But there are many factors in the contemporary church and culture which make it difficult for ministers to own the simple traditional understanding of the call with honesty and integrity. One of these has to do with the simple fact that Christianity is still the dominant religion in our society, and, therefore, heavily acculturated. I have been impressed, for example, with the depth and commitment of some American Zen Buddhist priests I have met. But to become a Zen priest in our culture necessitates a radical break in beliefs and life-style, and a rigor of discipline that is almost unknown in the Christian ministry. One can become a minister with minimal challenge to the cultural beliefs and life-styles of American society. And the discipline basically entails only three years of additional academic study and a change of employer.

The profundity of vocation proclaimed in the Bible and in tradition is also problematic for ministers because of the neglect of the inner life in American society. The depth of inner experience, and the quiet wisdom that needs a lifetime of spiritual practice to build, is almost as foreign to our churches as it is to the rest of our externalized, competitive, individualistic culture. But the most important obstacle to depth of vocation is the inexorable advance of scientific knowledge which undercuts the credibility and felt significance of Bible and tradition. Theology in the liberal mode has been preoccupied with this problem since the Enlightenment, attempting to find interstices in modern secularism where some aspects of the Christian myth might still survive, if not flourish. Such theological work has been essential to grounding a vocation while ministering in a secularized church to a secular culture. For the traditional understanding of the call presupposed a society which generally believed in traditional Christian doctrine, and honored the person who devoted his life to service according to that doctrine. But in contemporary society, the social supports for a traditional vocation are at best isolated and fragmented and, over the long run, are probably disappearing. It is out of this modern cultural change and erosion of the faith that the minister has to create a vocation that makes sense to the people he or she serves and that has integrity within the depths of his or her inner self. One can understand some of the recent thinking about models of ministry as efforts to help develop this intentionality.

Some clergy have grounded their intentionality in advocating social change. In the 1960s the gap between the pretensions and the realities of America's values became highly visible and inescapable for those who believe the Christian faith has to do essentially with the struggle for a more humane and just social order. But as Jeffrey Hadden documented in *The Gathering Storm in the Churches,* many clergy have developed a social change ministry partly as a result of uncertainty about traditional beliefs. Social change ministries made sense as an alternative grounding of their intentionality. Hadden concluded that the ministry is going through a crisis of identity, which "emerges out of the fact that the value system he has the responsibility of defining, sustaining, and transmitting is in a most serious state of flux."[9]

The professional model of ministry can be seen as another alternative grounding of intentionality. Remembering that the ministry was the original profession in Western Christendom, and indeed the source out of which other professions such as the law and teaching arose, James Glasse, in *Profession: Minister,* suggested that the minister reaffirm a vocational identity as a professional. Turning to the sociological literature, Glasse offered this definition of a professional:

> A professional is identified by five characteristics. (1) He is an *educated man,* master of some body of knowledge. The knowledge is not arcane and esoteric, but accessible to students in accredited educational institutions. (2) He is an *expert man,* master of some specific cluster of skills. These skills, while requiring some talent, can be learned and sharpened by practice under supervision. (3) He is an *institutional man,* relating himself to society and rendering his service through a historical social institution of which he is partly servant,

partly master. Even when he has a "private practice," he is a member of a professional association which has some control over his activities. (4) He is a *responsible man* who professes to be able to act competently in situations which require his services. He is committed to practice his profession according to high standards of competence and ethics. Finally, (5) he is a *dedicated man*. The professional characteristically "professes" something, some value for society. His dedication to the values of the profession is the ultimate basis of evaluation for his service.[10]

The model of the minister as a professional offers both opportunities and limitation to those seeking a coherent vocation. Every human being has an essential need and right to be competent—to do something well, and to know that he or she does it well. Along with the need to be loved and accepted unconditionally and to love and accept others without reservation, each person has the fundamental need to become an effective actor in the world, to be judged by and meet rigorous standards of appraisal and evaluation. Ministers are often unsure of themselves and their competence alongside the self-confidence of psychiatrists, psychologists, and other members of the helping professions who are developing new knowledge and applying it skillfully. What, after all, can the minister *do* and be proud of, assured that his or her contribution to the solution of the real problems of the world is on a par with those of the other professions?

However, the minister is not like other professionals who skillfully and authoritatively apply expert impersonal knowledge to individual clients and patients. The minister is fundamentally a person of faith, who has been grasped by the knowledge of the love of God and seeks to make that love known through his or her work. Intentionality in ministry is attenuated indeed if technical skills are its only base and it is not grounded in faith.

Intentionality as a sense of vocation has to be a

creative achievement of faith in our time, made more heroic by the lack of social role support and cultural acceptance. In such a situation, there are two dangers. One is that the minister will attempt to construct his or her own individual belief system and support for ministry. The other is the opposite—hiding behind a traditional belief or role without taking personal responsibility for it. As to the first danger, intentionality is not simply the minister's own vision. It is not an idiosyncratic creation of what constitutes the good life or a new social order or a new insight for spiritual growth. It is one person's reception of the ever-present revelation of Jesus Christ which comes to us in many different ways by means of the community of faith through the ages. Ministry does not belong to the individual minister, but to Jesus Christ. Recent form-critical studies of the New Testament demonstrate that it is the congregation or church as a whole that by grace participates in the ministry of Christ. Those passages about prophets, apostles, evangelists, etc., are not meant to delineate the order of different ministries but to illustrate how bountifully God has allowed the congregation to participate in the ministry of Christ.

On the other hand, every person must take personal responsibility for his or her professional or lay participation in the ministry of Jesus Christ. Everyone must own without proof or guarantee the possibility of a life of love lived in the presence of God, among the ambiguities of the created world. And yet it is not a personal creation. It is precisely a vision because it is beyond oneself and because it has been to some extent tested or negotiated with the tradition by which it has been received. It is, in fact, continually negotiated with the community of actual persons who proclaim by life and words the reality of Jesus Christ. The tradition of thought and creed, document and church order, is the cultural fruit of past

33

vision by which one can test to some extent the authenticity of one's own personal knowing of God.

It follows from what has been said that the minister does not possess the vision he or she negotiates, nor is he or she the embodiment of it. It is possible to enter the ministry partly as a way of evading difficulties in daily living, and to be captured by the image of the minister as one who is so possessed by the love of God as to be above the pain of interpersonal relationships and emotional problems. One can attempt to be merely a mouthpiece for the message of the gospel, or a role behind the clerical collar, or a benevolent authority giving the sacrament to the people. Even in this secular age, the things of God are powerful and numinous and should be approached with prayer and at least inward fasting. Otherwise one may be tempted to exchange the ambiguity of mortality for the false certainty of assumed divinity, and lose oneself in the process. And then one is of no help to those who come thirsting for the gospel in order to find a renewed humanity, not to escape from it. Carl Jung called this condition the inflation of the ego, and warned that it was an especial temptation for those whose work is with the deeper symbols of the psyche. Again, our cultural aversion to paying attention to the inner life, except as an indication of "mental illness," leaves us somewhat unprepared in these areas.

It is equally essential for parishioners to understand clearly that being a minister does not mean being a holy person who incarnates in every way what he or she commends. Ever since Martin Luther married and commended his marriage as an example to his followers, the parsonage has been oppressed by parishioners who expect not only the minister, but his or her spouse, marriage, children, and entire family to be an incarnate example of the love of God expressed in families. It is damaging enough for a minister to be trapped by such illusions. How much worse has it been for the minister's spouse who enters the marriage with no such pretensions but is held under and judged by those standards by the congregation. The minister is simply a man or a woman among other men and women, who is no better and no worse, not exempt in any way from any of the common conditions of humanity, but who has tasted a vision of the love of God and wishes to dedicate his or her professional life and skills to living out that vision and commending it to others.

SHARED INTENTIONALITY

For many ministers who at one time felt a strong vocation, and sustained a proactive work-style and a decision-making model, intentionality has faded over the years. Unlike the man quoted earlier, the second decade of their ministry finds them *less* able to carry out intentions and feeling more frustrated and futile in their work. One reason intentional ministries are lost is that they are carried out in isolation, each minister striving more or less alone to do an endless job against powerful resistance (usually internal as well as external). Firm resolve and heroic dedication are eventually undermined by this solitary struggle.

In contrast to this is the experience of people who begin to work together, to share their ministries (and often their lives), and who thereby gain both insight and support for intentionality. A recent pilot project in the professional development of young pastors[11] involved them in two years of regular cluster group meetings with other young pastors and a more experienced older man. Participants described the value of shared experience in several ways:

> Open discussion of how others responded to situations which I am now encountering was helpful.

I have grown in confidence and self-understanding, to see what once were debilitating problems as a challenge.

It has helped me accept my weaknesses as normal and my strengths as genuine assets.

I can be more honest about myself, my husband, our goals. I rely more on my own choices.

Helped to crystallize real and vital goals of my ministry.

The collegial group of clergy thus offers much support and concrete help to its members, helping to overcome the chronic tendency toward isolation in the ministry.

The intentional minister requires more than a supportive fellowship, however. She or he needs a *shared consciousness of the possibility of change,* what Paulo Freire terms *conscientização* in his book, *Pedagogy of the Oppressed.* Freire found that his literacy program among oppressed Brazilian peasants gave them not only reading skills but also a new hope that their life conditions could be changed. As the peasants worked together with Freire to identify the conditions which held them in bondage, the process led to the "emergence of consciousness and critical intervention in reality."[12] They became highly intentional rather than apathetic and reactive. In this new consciousness, they developed together "a climate of hope and confidence" in which limiting situations "appear as fetters [rather than] insurmountable barriers."[13] In the words of the young pastor just quoted, they saw "what once were debilitating problems as a challenge."

Intentional ministry thus requires *collaborative problem-solving,* working together to understand and change conditions not just to accept them. Its opposite is passive acceptance, or lonely futile striving in the face of massive cultural and personal pressures. One is reminded of the remarkable transformation of a few discouraged disciples of Jesus into a company of saints and apostles whose subsequent ministries were profoundly intentional. The Holy Spirit brought a new shared consciousness of the possibility of change.

Among Christians, among young people, among those working in liberating causes, with people trying to release their own potential, shared expectancy of change is well known. Many efforts exist today to create collegial or team ministries, church clusters, and even some Jesus communes as ways to shape the future actively together. Ministers attempting to be intentional about their ministries will find themselves unable to resist weariness of will and vocational corrosion without shared efforts to raise to consciousness the fundamental issues of ministry for collaborative problem-solving.

Just as it was impossible to discuss negotiation without mentioning intentionality, so our discussion of shared intentionality is a way of talking about effective negotiation. And the model of ministry we will apply in the rest of this book is a dialectic between these two necessary poles. Given this summary of the model, Thomas Campbell will in the next chapter describe the social systems with which the minister must negotiate. The present chapter closes with some self-appraisal questions for the minister who intends to be more intentional.

Since "being more intentional" may differ from one person-in-situation to another, the list of urgent issues and concerns demanding attention will vary. However, the following seven are proposed as operative for nearly every minister; you should add your own.

1. What is most important in my ministry?
   (What is my vocation, my mission?)

2. What is my own way of doing things, my *style* of working? (We are often not conscious of our style. It is not what we do but our characteristic way of going at it, which others may see better than we do.)

3. In the long run, where am I heading?
   (In personal life and in my ministry, what are my goals and priorities? What do I want to look back on twenty years from now?)

4. What do I do well?
   (Large or small successes in the past, skills enjoyed and rewarded, occasions of positive feedback, tasks completed well.)

5. What are my major resources, my support system, and how do I use them intentionally?
   (Resources include both supportive relationships with others and services from a variety of sources. The potential support system both for achieving goals and for managing stress is much larger than most clergy realize.)

6. What realities must I accept as limiting factors in my present situation?
   (Health, age, work environment, family circumstances, etc.)

7. Given my vocation and style, my goals, strengths and support system, and the reality factors which prevail, what kind (model) of ministry should I be carrying out?

The first six concerns build toward the seventh, which may be reworded: What are you primarily about in your present ministry? Are you above all trying to be an enabler of lay ministries, or an evangelizer of the unreached, or an advocate for the oppressed, or an instrument of healing for the sick, or is yours primarily a ministry of "presence" or of reconciliation or of organization? These are not only "varieties of gifts" but varieties also of ministry. They can be chosen wisely and fulfilled intentionally. There is much in our history, our theology, our churches, and ourselves which encourages reactivity and dependence. It is up to us to intend better together.

NOTES

1. Samuel Blizzard, "The Protestant Parish Minister's Integrating Roles," in Wayne E. Oates, ed., *The Minister's Own Mental Health* (Great Neck, N.Y.: Channel Press, 1961), pp. 144-45.

2. John E. Biersdorf, *Hunger for Experience: Vital Religious Communities in America* (New York: The Seabury Press, 1975), p. 16.

3. *Max Weber: Essays in Sociology*, trans. and ed. Hans H. Gerth and C. Wright Mills (New York: Oxford University Press, 1946).

4. Richard W. Bell and John P. Koval, "Collegiality: In the Priesthood," mimeographed (1971), p. 23.

5. *Ibid.*

6. Rollo May, *Love and Will* (New York: W. W. Norton & Co., 1969), pp. 223-25.

7. Urban T. Holmes, *The Future Shape of Ministry* (New York: The Seabury Press, 1971), p. 229.

8. *Ibid.*, pp. 92-93.

9. Jeffrey K. Hadden, *The Gathering Storm in the Churches* (Garden City, N.Y.: Doubleday & Co., 1969), p. 240.

10. James D. Glasse, *Profession: Minister* (Nashville: Abingdon Press, 1968), p. 38.

11. Mark A. Rouch, *Competent Ministry: A Guide to Effective Continuing Education* (Nashville: Abingdon Press, 1974), pp. 149-50 and n.

12. Paulo Freire, *Pedagogy of the Oppressed* (New York: The Seabury Press, 1971), p. 68.

13. *Ibid.*, p. 89.

Arenas of Negotiation

THOMAS C. CAMPBELL

INTRODUCTION

In this chapter, we will be setting intentionality within the context of the dominant reference groups with which the minister must negotiate, namely, the local congregation, the denomination, and the peer group. Each of these reference groups provides a situational element which must be taken seriously by the minister seeking to exercise intentionality concerning vocation.

The theme of the church as a voluntary association will continually reappear within the following analysis. For reasons which will be explicated below, the American church cannot be understood apart from the characteristics which are present within voluntary associations. It is not putting it too strongly to argue that no one should attempt to minister within American congregations who is not prepared to take the characteristics of voluntary associations seriously. It is our thesis that there is a creative and liberating way to conceptualize leadership within a voluntary association which enables productive development of intentionality.

The Minister as Negotiator

The preceding chapter made reference to the positive ways in which the term "professional" can be viewed by

Thomas C. Campbell is the academic vice-president and professor of theology and culture at United Theological Seminary, New Brighton, Minnesota.

a minister. Though there are many ways in which the ministry can be compared to other professions and can learn from them, there is yet a very distinct characteristic of the ministry in a voluntary church which differentiates it from most other professions. Other professions succeed as their special areas of expertise are expanded and protected against practice by nonprofessionals. The ministry is successful only if laypersons learn, understand, and integrate into their own lives that for which it stands. We have fulfilled our calling only when others know what we know, when we communicate to them the gospel of Jesus Christ, and when we have helped them to lead a more fulfilled life.

Therefore, in principle, we *must* negotiate with those who are related to our ministry. Sheer power relationships will not do, protection of our special concerns will not do, and being a "loner" will not produce effective ministry. Keeping this reason for affirming the value of negotiation in mind as we proceed to examine the various reference groups with which a minister deals will enable us to understand both the limiting factors present in the reference groups and the joyful possibilities which are there as well. Part of the paradoxical character of ministry is that we live in order that others too might live to the fullest!

THE LOCAL CONGREGATION
The American Context

As we have already noted, the local congregation in America is defined primarily by its voluntary character. Early in American history the separation of church and state was accepted as normative. Such a principle implies a religious pluralism and defines the church as a voluntary association. Several authors have developed in some detail the history and implications of voluntarism for the American church, and it is only necessary here to summarize some of the most important aspects of their work.

While it is true that American denominations differ in terms of their formal polity patterns, with some denominations having more formal centralized authority on either a presbyterial or an episcopal pattern, it is more significant to point to the fundamentally congregational polity which operates informally even within a non-congregational system. Bishops or presbyteries ignore the wishes of the local congregations on most matters only to their own detriment. The reasons are fairly obvious, for local church members are under no obligation to continue to belong to a particular congregation if the bishop or presbytery rules in some fashion which they are not willing to accept. More will be said on this matter in the section dealing with the denomination as reference group for the minister.

Studies have consistently shown that persons join voluntary churches for reasons which are not closely tied to the conscious theological traditions of the church chosen. They may join for reasons of ethnic loyalty, a sense of identity with the "type" of person found in the church, or they may "like" the minister. Potential members may evaluate the respective programs offered by competing congregations and make choices based on the reputed quality of the programs offered for children and youth, the quality of the music program, or the presence of certain social events in the life of the congregation. Also, potential members do not have strong denominational ties, and highly mobile persons have been shown to choose new churches on the basis of their own sense of status mobility.

The minister is thus faced with a congregation which has been drawn to membership in the church for very diverse reasons, only some of which may be easily identified with the content of the Christian faith. The minister must communicate (negotiate) with those who have willed to belong to that congregation. In this very process, he or she is faced with the issue of adaptation, for the Christian values must be translated in such a fashion that they reach the members at the level where their own motivations are operative. He or she cannot ignore the function of integration, for the diversity of gifts represented within the congregation need to be constantly harmonized and integrated one with the other.

The minister has goals of one sort or another for the congregation, whether they be in the realm of institutional success or social transformation of the larger culture. Those ministers who have lived through the 1960s have been particularly sensitized to the importance of social transformation. It became commonplace to refer to the church as mission, which did not mean the mission of evangelization of the neighborhood but rather the working for certain forms of social change. It was often assumed that if persons would work for such change they would necessarily become concerned with the Christian values. However, the minister was very often exhibiting a desire for change not shared by his or her congregation.

One very central reason for this disharmony is rooted in the same forces which produced the voluntary church. If one grants that there will be a pluralism of religious groupings in the culture and that there will be a separation of church and state, there is a strong press for religion to have its primary relation to the private concerns of life. Just exactly how a pluralism of religious bodies will exert force for social change except through the indirect influence of transformed individuals is very difficult to say.

The press toward "privatized" religion present from the very earliest years of our country has been strengthened by the growth of industrialization and bureaucratization within the country. People begin to see life as ever more specialized in its various areas of concern, and religion is more and more pressed into the area of private concern: home and family, personal ethics, and individual relation to the Divine Presence.

The American context is very much one of voluntary churches concerned primarily with private religious experience. What possible place can a minister's intentionality have in such a situation? We will answer this question by first examining the limiting factors present in the local voluntary congregation and will then examine the possibilities for intentionality which are present within this dominant reference group for the minister.

The Limiting Factors

1. Local Church Identification with Local Values

Although individuals in America do not spend a great deal of time examining the consistency of their personal value systems, there is a sense in which persons do develop a partially coherent system of values from which they function. Thus it would be highly unlikely that persons joining churches on a voluntary basis would leave behind their values in so doing. They are Americans, nationally oriented to see America as a country which sustained the hopes of their ancestors when they came to this "new land"; they are aware of flaws in that dream, but they are not sufficiently disenchanted to seek a new hope in some other country. Furthermore, residents of local neighborhoods and communities have by and large chosen their place of residence because they believe that the community in which they live is in some sense representative of themselves and the values for which they stand.

Thus at both the local and the national level the

members of congregations hold many values (often unconscious) which they bring with them into church membership. Will Herberg, Gibson Winter, Robert Brannon, and others have pointed to this identification of church members with cultural values, and they have lifted up in vivid fashion the limitations which such identification puts upon the acceptance of certain prophetic aspects of the Judeo-Christian heritage. It is very doubtful that a minister who is at severe odds with the value systems present in the area served by his or her church will find it an easy task to continue to encourage the church members to radically deny the values which they take for granted.

However, it would be a signal error to argue that local congregations are completely homogeneous in value orientation. Any minister who has served a congregation for more than a few months is as likely to be distressed by the heretogeneity of his or her congregation as by the homogeneity. There are dominant value orientations, age groups, and social status groups within any congregation, but these are rarely monolithic.

In a sense, then, the minister experiences the homogeneous character of the congregation as a limiting factor in negotiation to the extent that he or she sees himself or herself at odds with the dominant values in the congregation. However, it is also true that the heterogeneity of the congregation is seen as a limiting factor in negotiation to the extent that the minister is not willing to affirm the values of pluralism.

We will see how this paradoxical form of limitation in both homogeneity and heterogeneity can also be viewed as a possibility in negotiation.

2. Multiple Role Expectations Concerning the Clergy

Though there may be dominant value systems within a congregation, the members present the minister with a

46

wide spectrum of expectations concerning his or her role. In chapter 1 reference was made to Blizzard's studies on role expectation, and the researches of Glock and Stark have further shown how lay members of congregations see the minister as being responsible for a multi-faceted ministry.

To say that people with similar values will have different expectations of the clergy may appear inconsistent, but it is true nevertheless. Persons may well join a congregation because it upholds their values, or they think it does, but they also expect the congregation and its minister to work for changes which they sense are needed, and furthermore the individual members are rarely persons without places of personal pain and anguish. In the midst of such conflicting desires, the minister is expected both to challenge and to provide comfort.

The minister does not need to be told how multiple role expectations are experienced as a limiting factor in ministry, and it is naïve to argue that a personal sense of intentionality will radically change them. It is appropriate to speak of one's own basic strengths and weaknesses in relation to the multiple roles expected, but it is inappropriate to argue that certain roles can be completely eliminated through intentionality. If one does not have some desire for diversity of functional roles, then one probably should not attempt to exercise leadership in a voluntary church institution. Multiple expectations put some limits on the intentionality of all ministers, but they also put limits on the kinds of persons who should seek to be clergy.

3. The Minister as Person

In addition to the limits imposed by the value systems of the parishioners, and the multiple role expectations, the minister him-or herself has been conditioned by his or her own past experiences in childhood and youth. James Dittes has convincingly shown that many ministers have grown up with the pattern of being "little adults." They tended to be firstborn or only children, they identified early with adult values, they tended to excel in individual rather than team sports, and they tended to be elected to leadership offices where they functioned between the peer world and the adult world.

Such a conditioning has made the minister very sensitive to being put "on the spot" between conflicting groups. The seminary told him or her not to accept the values which the congregation affirms, the congregation tells him or her not to accept the programs which are fostered by national agencies, and lay individuals and subgroups tell him or her to perform too many roles! With such a wide set of limiting factors, what can possibly be said? Let us examine each of the factors which we have delineated to find out if they are all as limiting as they seem at first glance.

Possibilities Within the Context

1. Differential and Partial Identification of the Laity

Ministers are well aware of the laity's cultural identifications, and may well be overwhelmed by them. However, the voluntary church has a significant advantage which is often overlooked as we become immersed in its limitations. Unlike an organization in which the very livelihood of the participants is involved, the constituents of a voluntary association only partially identify with the organization, and flow in and out of membership. At first glance that may seem to be a further limiting factor, but, on the contrary, such fluidity and partial identification is a significant basis for creative ministry.

A minister who understands the character of a

voluntary association will see that, though people may disagree with certain aspects of his or her intentional ministry, they are free to identify to the extent that they see fit. Thus, over time, the minister is able to build a constituency which shares his or her views of the purposes of the Christian faith, and in the process he or she need not disrupt the lives of the people who do not share the same intentionality. Any minister whose predecessor has served the parish for ten years or more can see the very way in which the congregation has taken on the "coloring" of its minister. The new minister is often frustrated by the patterns which have been established, but, in fact, they should be seen as an encouraging sign that it is quite possible to influence the style and life experiences of a voluntary association, even though this will rarely be accomplished in a few months.

Furthermore, partial identification with voluntary churches means that the church will affect different types of participants in different ways. Studies by Quinley; Glock, Ringer, and Babbie; and Campbell and Fukuyama have shown that the differential participation of members is correlated with different consequences of church participation. Too often we have divided church participation into the broad categories of national opinion surveys, submerging the subtle differences which we uncover when we look at the different subgroups that make up a church.

The intentional minister recognizes the differential way in which laity respond to church programs, and sets goals for ministry which are appropriate to the different forms of participation present within the congregation. He or she does not expect all participants to agree with all that other persons are doing in the life of the church, but he or she does expect them to recognize that persons

49

have different needs and will relate to the congregation through different programs and on different levels.

Negotiation need not be in the form of confrontation, but it may well be expressed in terms of recognizing felt needs and allowing "space" within the church program to address those needs. The minister of a voluntary church need not enthusiastically promote all programs addressed to all needs, but he or she can allow for the expression of such needs. Such "allowance" is a form of negotiation and normally results in more allowance on the part of the parishioners for the minister to develop other programs not so readily recognized as being needed.

Earlier we spoke of the predominant homogeneity and subordinate heterogeneity within most American congregations. The homogeneity can be viewed as a possibility for negotiation, since it enables the minister to have a relatively precise sense of the values of the group with which he or she is negotiating. Too often clergy have neglected such precision in viewing a congregation. Time spent evaluating the social scene from which the particular congregation is drawn will pay enormous dividends in terms of understanding the dominant myths and realities which inform a particular group of laity. For example, it is highly unlikely that a doctrine of lay vocation will be easily understood by a blue-collar congregation which views "work" as simply a necessary evil. "Vocation" is more easily understood in terms of the appropriate use of leisure time. Likewise a minister in a very privileged congregation can expect a ready acceptance of the view that one's profession should be seen as a calling and a vocation. At the same time he or she is likely to experience considerable resistance to increased requests for the use of "free time" for various and sundry "good Christian causes." In our time, the Veblen thesis of the "leisure class" has been turned on its head! The more most persons climb the social ladder, the less opportunity they have for "free" use of time.

Contrariwise, the more heterogeneous a congregation is in value and social orientation, the more the minister is able to negotiate new models for mission based on the pluralism of populations within the community of believers. He or she is able to develop a strong model of multiple ministries which aid, correct, support, and critique one another. Such a pattern of negotiation necessitates a minister who does not see his or her theological and social understandings as normative for all humankind.

In summary, strong homogeneity in a congregation directs the minister toward one form of negotiating style, while predominant heterogeneity suggests a different form for negotiating. In all probability, most congregations are predominantly homogeneous with secondary heterogeneity, and the minister will have a chance to explore the possibilities of negotiating from both perspectives.

2. The Creative Parson

Multiple role expectations for clergy are likewise an opportunity for creative negotiation. To assume that the minister of a contemporary congregation cannot be a one-talent or one-role professional is not to assume that all role expectations are necessarily of equal importance, either to the minister or to the congregation.

It is sheer arrogance for any one minister to assume that he or she has equal gifts in all realms. A congregation will not admire such a person; they may seem to, but over time they will see the flaws in the minister's self-awareness and will treat his or her sense of perfection with disdain. Honest self-appraisal not only aids the negotiating task but enables the church membership to gain a new awareness of their own limitations and gifts. Leveling with a church council is rarely received with hostility unless the minister begins by pointing up the limitations of the council rather than his or her own limitations.

Finally, a minister often interprets "negotiation" as a means of convincing the congregation of the superiority of his or her own point of view. "Negotiation" as it is being used here is not a synonym for "soft-sell prophecy," but rather it is honest give and take. How deeply does the minister really integrate his or her acceptance of the doctrine of the priesthood of all believers? Too often what is meant by such a doctrine is that the laity should begin to take on the coloration and viewpoints of the clergy. The fuller meaning is that even the fully trained seminary graduate does not have a monopoly on theological truth, and the local barber just could better understand the depths of the Christian truths. The laity quickly evaluate the extent to which the minister honestly accepts their gifts and interpretations as being of worth or not. For the minister, to accept the fundamental worth of someone he or she differs with is not to become an ecclesiastical chameleon; it is a fundamental affirmation of both the height and the depth of the Christian doctrine of the human person.

3. Making Decisions About Ministry

That certain types of persons with certain predominant social histories are selectively drawn to parish ministry is in one sense a limiting factor which must be fought against in the name of Christian freedom and creativity. However, the fact of selective recruitment for parish ministry is also an opportunity for more clearly understanding the meaning of ordination and the proper functions of professional religious leadership.

This author's theology of ordination does not assume any form of hierarchical worth. The professional ministry is at the most basic level an office. Not all persons are called to that office, nor should they be. And while a sense of personal calling is essential to professional ministry, it is also essential to full Christian life. Some persons may feel threatened by the argument that all members of the Body of Christ have equal worth in principle, but others find such an affirmation freeing. Therefore, when I read studies such as *Ex-Pastors* by Jud, Mills, and Burch, I accept that there are indeed some problems to be faced in the life of the church when its professional leaders choose to leave the ministry, but equally I rejoice that those who have not found fulfillment in the ministry have not in any way lost the sense of personal Christian calling. If one finds most satisfaction in working with systems and larger social groupings, then a church with socially conditioned tendencies toward privatized religious experience will be overly frustrating. (More will be said below about the matter of denominational officials.) If one does not find satisfaction in interpersonal encounter, then one ought not to accept the office of ministry as the place of one's Christian calling.

As both a seminary educator and one concerned about the ongoing life of the churches, I believe that, rather than too much mobility in and out of seminaries and churches, we do not have enough. Sorting out personal strengths and weaknesses is a very complex matter in our highly specialized culture, and I can only support the increased use of career development centers as a normative experience both during and after seminary education. Finding that moment of joy when one has established a satisfying sense of "fit" with one's environment is a creative event. And just as one does not hope for the Second Coming tomorrow morning but sees the creative possibilities in tolerable ambiguity, so the sense of "fit" is not to be seen as final and as confining, but rather as being filled with exciting ambiguity.

To know what it is to be "on the spot," in Dittes' phrase, is to be a representative human. We are all on the spot of hearing conflicting demands, and to have personally known the pain *and* joy of such a position is to be capable of true ministry to others, aiding them in their pain and supporting them in their joys.

Functioning Within the Local Context

One can bemoan the localized values, or minister to and through them. One can see homogeneous values as limiting creativity or as a means for aiding productive consensus. One can see heterogeneity of values in the congregation as hopeless confusion or as an opportunity to utilize conflict to reach deeper insights. One can see socially conditioned selective recruitment of membership as an evil power of the social order, or one can see it as an opportunity to build an intentionalized congregation over time. One can despair about the extent to which clergy either fit a pattern or deviate from it, or one can rejoice that one's social history has prepared one for a very particular calling and at the same time has allowed one to deviate sufficiently from the norm to be of real value to one's own congregation.

THE DENOMINATION AS NEGOTIATING CENTER

The American Context

It is by now common knowledge that just as local congregations tend to draw selectively from the total American population, so too, for reasons of voluntary church participation, do denominations. Several sociological studies have been able to rank the various denominations according to social class variables cross-related to ethnic and racial groupings. H. Richard Niebuhr's *Social Sources of Denominationalism,* while old in terms of years, reads as though it were written yesterday. These social conditioning forces are very powerful and persistent.

A second set of forces which needs to be lifted up when considering denominations concerns church polity. Although the American scene is predominantly characterized by congregational polity, there are nevertheless secondary influences stemming from more hierarchically or presbyterially organized church systems. Just as one could argue that all formal bishops are limited by fundamentally congregational churches, so too it is appropriate to note that all congregational "executives" have major forms of informal power. One can argue, as we have, that presbyteries can legislate only limited authority upon local churches, yet the most independent congregation looks to *some* representational body for a sense of congregational identity. With the qualifications just noted, Paul Harrison's study entitled *Authority and Power in the Free Church Tradition* holds true of most American churches. Tradition is only the mimicking of recent history, clerical authority is heavily dependent on personal "charisma," and bureaucracies are not fully rationalized.

When speaking of denominational centers of power, it is appropriate to mention also the studies which have been done of persons in the specialized ministries. Hammond in *The Campus Clergyman,* Underwood in his study of the campus ministry, and Mills in his studies of "ex-pastors" in bureaucratic roles, all tend to affirm that selective recruitment does function here as well as in the ministry in general. It is not the case that denominations are organized in such a way that persons who are strongly supportive of local church ministry come to major places of authority and power. This may be a "limiting" factor in negotiating with denominations, and it also may be a form of "possibility." More will be said later on this issue.

Finally, denominations are a major form of "reward system" for practicing ministers. In a social order as complex as the contemporary American one, mobility is to some extent dependent on national organization. It may or may not function effectively, but ministers are most likely to find some form of connectional system beneficial when mobility is desired.

The Limiting Context

Denominational offices *do* put both formal and informal pressure upon local churches to function in ways which may not be the most comfortable for them or their clergy leaders. Denominational officers and bodies may take unpopular social stands, they may request seemingly endless new funds for national and regional mission priorities, and they may appear out of touch with the "true" local issues. For any professional who believes that the local ministry should respond only to the needs of local and privatized congregations, this pressure manifests itself as a limitation on ministry.

Seminaries, often identified with denominations, likewise appear to set impossible limitations on ministry. They suggest ideals which are difficult if not impossible in practice, they continually advocate some form of continuing education, they hold out the model of specialized theological competence as *the* model for ministry, and they need money.

In the midst of these denominationally related pressures, the minister is faced with another source of tension. For better or for worse, denominational identification is normative for American Christianity, and identity for ministers is related to denominational affiliation. Denominations are in a sense the ministers' "party caucus" within Christianity. Many ministers are uneasy about such identification. They are well aware that they do not agree with all that the denomination actually stands for, and certainly not with all that it is popularly believed to stand for; and yet it is a convenient general place within which to place oneself. Ministers like to see the denomination as a necessary evil. Bureaucrats are bureaucrats even when they are ordained, largely uncomprehending of local problems even when they use "God talk," and most seminary professors or denominational leaders, ministers suspect, would not last for more than a few weeks if they were out on the "firing line."

Possibilities Within the Context

In *Small Town in Mass Society* Vidich and Bensman used the image of the "gatekeeper" to describe the role of school superintendents, county agents, and local ministers. According to the authors, these are all persons who have some credentials in the larger society, understand something of how one gets what one needs from the larger society, and act as a channel of communication between their own organizations and larger social bodies.

It is not too unfair to Vidich and Bensman's image to suggest that this definition of a "gatekeeper" is a good description of a "negotiator." The negotiator is somewhere between two parties and at the same time has some agenda of his or her own. A school superintendent who desires an upgrading of curricular offerings is in a good position with respect to his or her school board if the board is only likely to accredit stronger curricula. A minister who sees the need for the congregation to broaden its horizons beyond Main Street is aided by having access to interpreters who are willing to come to the church to present the larger needs of world mission.

He or she is aided by a denominational policy on compensation when the local constituency is faced with a leaking roof.

On the other hand, the local pressures present the minister with leverage to negotiate for the development of programs of which the national church may be only dimly aware.

The gatekeeper-negotiator is indeed pressed by conflicting expectations between local and denominational priorities, but such pressure is one of the major sources for creative renewal. My own feeling is that human sin and finitude encourage most of us ministers to become too comfortable within the institutional role we fulfill, and the plurality of "centers" with which we must negotiate to accomplish our goals contributes to a dynamic that is essential for responsible action.

While the denomination as "caucus" means that we will always need to develop compromises in order to satisfy the several subparties which make up the caucus, it also means that more resources can be brought to bear upon the issues and that myopic visions will be enlarged.

It is not popular in contemporary society to uphold the liberal vision of the benefits of pluralism, but I can only confess to having a greater fear of unrestrained self-interest than of the delays and compromises which are the inevitable result of appealing to larger governing centers for decision-making and program policy.

In the 1960s there was too much agenda-setting by denominational offices and bureaucracies, but there is a danger that in the current period we may fail to acknowledge the appropriate role for larger bodies than the local congregations. The minister can be an effective negotiator in this process of local-denominational relations. He or she has a "constituency" to contribute and must be taken seriously. Likewise, he or she is also committed to larger than local concerns and can speak for those concerns by virtue of his or her denominational identity.

PEERS AS A NEGOTIATING CENTER

The American Context

There have been several efforts in recent years to develop strong professional associations among clergy. Those who advocate such associations point to other professions and argue for associations as a means to self-esteem within the profession. Given the priority of voluntary associations in American society, it is not surprising that professional associations have emerged as broadly as they have. However, one ingredient is lacking which affects the possibility of strong professional associations among clergy. Clergy do not have a monopoly in terms of services rendered. The state is not willing to support any effort for a clerical monopoly, and in principle any person can claim to be a minister by simply organizing some supporting and validating body. Graduate professional degrees notwithstanding, clergy have their basic validation not from fellow clergy but through the constituency of the church they serve (or its denomination). Many denominations include laity in the process of ordination. For these reasons the reward and punishment system for clergy is fundamentally within the church not the professional association of peers.

The Limiting Context

Professional peers do not contribute the strongest form of validation for clergy, for the reasons stated above. The relative social status of ministers in this country depends more on the social status of the church served than on the role performed. The peers, therefore, are not seen as the primary negotiating group for ministers, and much more self-interest is served through negotiation with local congregations and denominations.

Possibilities Within the Context

The very fact that the peer group is such a weak system for rewards and punishments does not eliminate its value. Indeed, considerable evidence has emerged within recent years to show that the clergy are increasingly turning to peer groups for personal growth, personal support, and intimacy. With the peer group, drawn together on an ad hoc basis, the minister is able to share joys and sorrows, ideas and failures, frustrations and visions. Precisely because this group holds so little of the rewards and punishments of the "system," it enables sharing without fear of repercussions.

It is probably an overstatement to say that the minister negotiates with such a peer group in the same way as he or she negotiates with the local congregation and the denomination. However, risking sharing of one's ideas and failures is a form of negotiation which may well be the prelude to honest negotiation within these other two reference groups. In a voluntary peer group the minister is relating to a very narrow group defined through self-selection processes, and it can provide very low threat and very great personal support.

THE INTENTIONAL MINISTER
AND NEGOTIATING CENTERS

This chapter has had as its focus an examination of the major reference groups with which the minister as professional negotiates. It has attempted to answer two of the questions which closed the previous chapter: What are my major resources, and what are the realities I must accept as limiting factors in my present situation?

In summary, I have tried to show how reference groups can be viewed both as limiting and as resources of possibility. What tends to be seen as a limitation can be constructively viewed as an opportunity without denying the fact of limitation. This is a paradoxical reality which faces the minister, and yet naming the paradox is the first step in the development of negotiating skills.

The minister negotiates first and foremost with the local congregation, secondarily with the denomination, and only in a tertiary way with the peer group.

For the minister who wants to develop negotiating skills, the place to begin may well be with the peers. They know the strains and the joys and can reinforce negotiating skills which are in the process of development.

BIBLIOGRAPHY

Brannon, R. C. L. "Organizational Vulnerability in Modern Religious Organizations." *Journal for the Scientific Study of Religion,* vol. 10, no. 1 (Spring, 1971), pp. 27-32.

Campbell, T. C., and Fukuyama, Y. *The Fragmented Layman.* Philadelphia: Pilgrim Press, 1970.

Dittes, James. *Minister on the Spot.* Philadelphia: Pilgrim Press, 1970.

Glock, C.; Ringer, B.; and Babbie, E. *To Comfort and to Challenge.* Berkeley: University of California Press, 1967.

Glock, C., and Stark, R. *Religion and Society in Tension.* Chicago: Rand McNally & Co., 1965.

Hammond, Philip. *The Campus Clergyman.* New York: Basic Books, 1966.

Harrison, Paul. *Authority and Power in the Free Church Tradition.* Carbondale: Southern Illinois University Press [1959], 1971.

Herberg, Will. *Protestant, Catholic, Jew.* Garden City, N.Y.: Doubleday & Co., 1960.

Jud, G.; Mills, E. W.; and Burch, G. *Ex-Pastors.* Philadelphia: Pilgrim Press, 1970.

Niebuhr, H. R. *The Social Sources of Denominationalism.* Meridian Books; Cleveland: World Publishing Co. [1929], 1957.

Quinley, H. "Hawks and Doves Among the Clergy." *Ministry Studies,* vol. 3, no. 3 (October, 1969), pp. 5-20.

Underwood, K., ed. *The Church, The University, and Social Policy.* Middletown, Conn.: Wesleyan University Press, 1969.

Vidich, A., and Bensman, J. *Small Town in Mass Society.* Princeton: Princeton University Press [1960], 1968.

Winter, G. *Suburban Captivity of the Churches.* New York: The Macmillan Co. [1961], 1962.

PART II

TAKING CHARGE OF YOUR CAREER

One fundamental arena in which to negotiate an intentional ministry is your career. That lifelong trajectory of hopes, work, celebration, and concern for God's mission needs to be intentional if it is to be faithful and effective. And it needs to be continually negotiated and renegotiated: for it is not a solitary trek, but a pilgrimage with many companions who powerfully influence its direction and quality. The first chapter in this part presents a useful framework for career planning which comes from much research and clinical experience in career counseling centers for clergy. The second chapter addresses the concrete step of getting a job, and the third is devoted to helpful counseling for that lifelong process of learning called professional theological education.

Career Planning

THOMAS E. BROWN

"Intentionality is the structure which gives meaning to experience. Our intentions are decisive with respect to how we perceive the world." "But," Rollo May goes on to say, "this is only one side of intentionality. The other side is that it also does come from the object. Intentionality is the bridge between these. It is the structure of meaning which makes it possible for us, subjects that we are, to see and understand the outside world, objective as it is. In intentionality, the dichotomy between subject and object is partially overcome."[1]

As has been pointed elsewhere in this volume, the religious leader in the modern church and the modern world has a great need to be intentional about his or her role and work. Historical analysis would support the statement that such has always been the case with those who have been effective in religious leadership, but since that is not within the purpose of this chapter, the emphasis here will be upon the minister of today.

Concern for intentionality is not simply personal; it is also organizational, societal, and professional. The concern for a sense of direction, or, more correctly, a "reason for being," permeates human culture today. Thus, the religious leader must strive to find leadership

Thomas E. Brown was the director of the Northeast Career Center, Princeton, New Jersey, and is currently the director of the career counseling facilities at Lancaster Theological Seminary, Lancaster, Pennsylvania.

roles which enable religious organizations to develop intentionality and which assist in the struggles of other kinds of communities to do likewise. He or she must also directly intervene in the individual searches for meaning that persons are carrying out. Since modern man's various crises—of identity, of faith, racial, national—might be summarized in the term "crisis of intentionality," the religious leader knowingly or unknowingly is addressing himself or herself to the question of intentionality.

To do this without knowing how to deal with one's own intentionality is to act out the classic "blind leading the blind" syndrome. Sensitive and concerned religious leaders are thus anxious to deal with their own intentionality, knowing as they do, that, in the words of Rabbi Martin Siegel,

> the old gods are dead, gone. New ways to worship need to be discovered. Man must find a new vocabulary for his religious reality. He needs new understanding, new meanings, and new expressions of God. As it is, he is only running from himself, cloaking fears and self doubts in hectic activity, afraid to plunge into himself to learn what he really feels, and resisting his own consciousness. And where through all of this is God? God is just some venerated anachronism grandfather used to pray to.
>
> And here I am, Rabbi Martin Siegel, keeping myself alive and earning a living (the phrase strikes me harshly) by preserving an institution in which God has grown meaningless. Yet I know that the life I've had given me can't be satisfied by working furiously on the fringe of things. I want to be where people live.
>
> I came here to create, not to cremate. But I know I am presiding over the last dying flame of a once great institution, offering tidbits of consolation to make the demise all the less painful. But nobody cares. Why do I bother?[2]

"Why do I bother?" That is the question for Martin Siegel, and when he raises it again near the end of his

diary he reminds the reader of the questions he raised when he was ordained: "Suddenly, I was no longer Martin Siegel. I was the *Rabbi. The Rabbi?* I thought. *What is the Rabbi? Who is the Rabbi? What is the Rabbi supposed to be? Why am I the Rabbi?"* [3]

Such questions must and do engage the minds and emotions, and absorb great portions of the meditative life, of large numbers of religious leaders today. Some change their occupations in response, though often only after years of struggle; others return to seminary for "another shot in the arm"; yet others try every new technique, idea, program, and fad that comes along. Some go to career-development centers seeking guidance through that process; some spend years in psychoanalysis engaging in the same search; some are constantly asking their superiors, or denominations, or laity, or colleagues, for the answers. Some search the Scriptures hoping for answers which have practical as well as philosophical relevance. Some engage their spouses in endless dialogue, hoping that such questions will once and for all be laid to rest. Some do all of these things and more. Yet the questions remain and the search continues.

Many, of course, realize, as Martin Siegel realizes, that the questions will not be finally answered, for *intentionality is not an end goal.* For the dynamic religious leader, as for any other person, it is a never-ending process. Struggling with intentionality is a way of life for the alive person; thus May is able to say that "the degree of intentionality can define the aliveness of the person," to quote Paul Tillich's statement in *The Courage to Be* that "man's vitality is as great as his intentionality: they are interdependent," and to indicate that "intentionality is the constructive use of normal anxiety." [4]

How should one process the effort to be intentional, then? The rest of this chapter will be devoted to answering that question, specifically with respect to the professional development of the practicing religious leader, but in a way that is relevant to the life of any man or woman who is involved in *profession*.

The concepts presented are based upon vocational counseling, occupational psychology, and career-development theories and practice, interpreted according to their use by the writer in individual and group counseling practice with several thousand clergy, nuns, church educators, and church administrators.

INTENTIONALITY AND THE INTEGRATIVE COMPROMISE

We began with a statement by Rollo May which interprets intentionality as a bridge between the inside world of the individual and the outside world, between subject and object. In occupational decision-making, whatever process is followed must provide the individual with information about himself or herself (inside world) and about the realities outside the individual (object world). Moreover, the process must provide a method for linking these in a way that makes sense for the life of the individual. Thus, the objective of occupational counseling and planning is to find that compromise between self and world which is integrative, which helps the individual's life take on a more holistic perspective as a result. This "integrative compromise"[5] may thus be seen as the combination of *functional decisions* which enable intentionality to be acted out through professional roles, occupational choices, and life decisions of all kinds. The compromises, though, are not simply between the self and the object world; they are also necessary for the effective management of internal conflicts and for the discovery of potentialities that exist in internal complementarities.

This is easiest to understand if the individual is thought of as a complex mixture of *factor sets:* abilities, knowledge, values, interests, needs or drives, and behavioral characteristics. These terms will be defined in brief detail later; at this point it is important to note that we can describe them in separate factor sets only in an abstract view of the human personality. In real persons they overlap and intermesh in ways that often discourage efforts to discover and consider them separately. This accounts for much of the single-factor decision-making which is reflected through occupational and developmental decisions. It also accounts for much of the dissatisfaction individuals feel in response to work endeavors, the disappointment with the results of various continuing education efforts, the ineffective performance which occurs in spite of extensive preparation to enter a field and intensive professional development efforts along the way.

Consider the case of the young minister who, because of his abilities, interests, and values, devoted most of his seminary effort to learning concepts and skills related to preaching, counseling, and teaching. Obtaining a staff position in a large congregation, he discovered that his personality was well suited to these roles. He found himself engaging in them with enthusiasm, increasing, through practice and through dialogue with colleagues, his skills and knowledge relative to them. The role demands and the situation were very fulfilling to his needs, until two things happened: a change of senior pastors resulted in fewer opportunities to preach, and his own growing family added to the pressure to move into a "pastorate of my own" in order to increase income. Thus, he sought and received a call to a pastorate in which opportunity to preach was regular, counseling was needed, and teaching would be appreciated: a congregation on the edge of a college campus. He sought career counseling in order to plan how to become an administrator, since he realized that this would be required of him as the only pastor. Yet he knew himself well enough to be afraid of the administrative role. He sensed what the career evaluation was to confirm: his characteristics, interests, and abilities were all contrary to administrative endeavors. But as he was bright enough to learn almost any ability, he felt he *should* become an effective administrator in order to be "satisfactory" in performance, even if it meant sacrificing a great deal of satisfaction. While such would obviously not always be the case, it became clear to him, as well as to the counselor, that this approach would be a *dis*-integrative compromise for him. Predictive data indicated that the required study would probably be detrimental to the performance of his best roles and the administrative activities would probably reward him negatively.

In a setting in which the importance of the integrative compromise is disregarded, the "tyranny of the should" [6] would have functioned and he would have compromised self in a probably destructive way in order to fulfill internal and external demands. Instead, he was encouraged to negotiate with the reality outside himself—the church board—and to try to discover suitable alternative ways to administer the congregation. Hesitantly he approached the church board and found to his surprise and pleasure that they were quite sensitive to his concern and more than ready to cooperate in his plan. He reported that they indicated that they were so because they were impressed by his sense of self-understanding and -direction. His intentionality, as expressed through a statement of role abilities and preferences and how these would benefit the congregation more if used without spending energy in administration, encouraged them to search for alternatives. He was careful, too, not to demean or devalue administration simply because it was not for him. He pursued his ministry in that congregation with a high sense of satisfaction and satisfactoriness, and engaged in continuing education in the areas of preaching and counseling while he was there.

Another case which sets this one in perspective is that of a church program administrator who pursued counseling as his continuing education emphasis. In fact, he obtained a doctorate in the field, underwent a great deal of therapy while in graduate school, and then proceeded to seek and hold positions which called for administrative skills. Only when he had gotten close to full-time practice in counseling did he realize that his doctoral study had been in a field in which he had little interest, which he did not value highly, and for which his personality was ill suited in spite of training and therapy. He was middle-aged by the time he came to realize that while he had planned his continuing education according to a disintegrative compromise, he had fortunately corrected his direction at the point of full employment.

Oversimplified in brief illustration, these two cases nevertheless exemplify with positive outcomes the significance of integrative compromise between internal factors as well as between the internal and external. Not all are so fortunate as these two, and frequently disintegrative compromises are acted out for years with predictable impact on all involved. They frequently lead to crises of major proportion for the individual minister[7] if not for the congregations and other organizations for which such persons work. They also demonstrate that occupational choice is "a life-long process in which the individual seeks to find the optimal fit between his career preparation and goals and the realities of the world of work."[8]

71

SOME CLARIFYING DEFINITIONS

Several of the terms used in this discussion do not always mean the same thing to different users. This is particularly true of *career, occupation,* and *vocation,* which are often considered synonyms for work or work life. Specialists in the fields of occupational psychology and occupational sociology sometimes distinguish between "occupation" and "career" by describing the present "job" as an "occupation," and "career" as a series of occupations. Alternatively, "career" means "profession" as distinct from leisure time activity, family life, etc. The word "vocation" is often used to refer to any one of these, or to all of them as a group. Church-related persons, however, frequently restrict "vocation" to that which is done in response to a felt "call" from God and/or the church. In Catholic communities the word refers most frequently to that which has to do with religion, with full life in religion, though it is undergoing some change in meaning among Roman Catholics owing to the radical changes since Vatican II. One may now have a religious *vocation* without spending one's whole life in a religious community or at a specifically religious task, and, as previously, the term is still used to refer to the married or single state.

Considering this variety of usage, it may be helpful to state explicitly what we mean by these words, as we use them in this chapter.

An *occupation* is a *field of endeavor*—a trade, craft, or profession—in which one works "for a living." It distinguishes between fields in broad groupings which have common characteristics. Examples of occupations are the ministry, teaching, carpentry, engineering, law, medicine, music, painting, journalism.

Jobs or *positions* define roles or sets of roles within an occupation. *Roles* refer to the functions or tasks to be performed.

72

There are also *suboccupations,* which are more narrow in comprehensiveness than occupation, but broader than jobs or positions.

This outline, read from left to right, serves to illustrate the distinctions:

Occupation	Suboccupation	Job/Position
Ministry	Parish pastor	Pastor, "First Church"
Ministry	Christian educator	Director of education
Teaching	Primary teacher	Teacher, third grade
Medicine	Family physician	Private practice
Engineering	Chemical engineer	Laboratory manager
Law	Corporation lawyer	Counsel, "ABC Corp."
Carpentry	Cabinetmaker	Foreman, "Cabinets, Inc."

A *career* is the continuum along which a person lives out his or her occupational life. Thus, *each person has only one career:* the stream of life moving chronologically, along which one may have one occupation, or a series of them; one position within an occupation, or several suboccupations or jobs. Career development, therefore, refers to much more than occupational choice, or job training, or professional development. *It refers to the life development which enables a person to live out the occupational aspect of the life continuum with greater satisfaction and satisfactoriness.* The continuum may be radically altered a number of times along the way, but it remains *one* career.

Vocation is different from career in that it refers to the *whole of life:* vocation is the individual's *response to the call to live.* Career development, comprehensive as it might be in terms of involvement with most, if not all, the life factors in an individual situation, nevertheless is much more narrow than vocational development. Vocation includes the other contexts of life: family, religion, friendships, community, leisure, and such.

While these distinctions may not seem to be very important, they are very helpful when it comes to (a) distinguishing between various types of counseling and counselors and (b) helping an individual look at his or her life in its totality, with a concern for the interrelationships between contexts, for a comprehensive approach to life planning as well as to career planning. Career counseling and career development planning need to take place in a vocational framework, just as job counseling or occupational decision-making needs to be considered in a career development framework.

Chart 1 illustrates the comprehensiveness of the linguistic relationships being described, though it must be kept in mind that life is never as "cleanly drawn" as this. The life pattern of a particular individual would

CHART 1
A Schema of Vocational Dynamics[9]

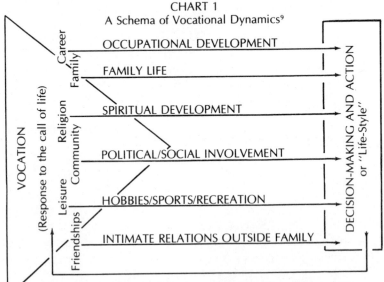

As the drawing implies, in a *dynamic* life system what happens in the *life-style*, or "mixing tank," flows back to influence vocation, and thus to effect what happens on each of the continua flowing out as expressions of vocation.

show the lines weaving in and out of each other, with all manner of interconnections, confusions, conflicts, and disjunctures; and, of course, for some persons the listing of contexts would be different, with some added that are not shown here and some which are shown here being disregarded. In choosing these six contexts, however, an effort was made to be comprehensive about life.

We mentioned earlier that in the process of making occupational choices an individual engages in internal as well as external compromises. We pointed out that this is most easily understood if the functional person is thought of as being composed of sets of distinctive factors described as abilities, knowledge, values, interests, needs or drives, and personality characteristics. These terms also require definition.

> *Abilities.* Abilities are enablers of function, such as the basic abilities of intellectual power, creativity, artistic sensitivity, or those "tools" available for use such as the ability to observe, research, analyze, develop ideas, mentor, teach, supervise, manage, speak, design, build, repair, and so on.
>
> *Knowledge.* Knowledge refers to the mastered sets of content essential to use of abilities and the fulfillment of roles: to *research* the Bible, for example, one needs historical, linguistic and other data as knowledge which is possessed or available; to *repair* a machine, one needs knowledge of its theory of operation, its parts, etc.
>
> *Values.* Values are the commitments, priorities, "judgment guides" held within the person: faith in God, commitment to Christ, family, church, money, power, service, community, justice, etc.
>
> *Interests.* Interests represent the attraction felt to the variety of activities possible in life: for instance, reading, walking, speaking, serving, adventuring, singing, listening.
>
> *Needs or Drives.* Needs are the desires within the person which strive for satisfaction: autonomy, achievement, intimacy, compensation, responsibility, recognition, and others.

Personality Characteristics. Characteristics are behavioral-dynamic variables which influence how abilities are used, or values fulfilled or needs met: extraversion, dominance, self-confidence, conscientiousness, trust, forthrightness, for example.[10]

A third set of definitions will complete this section and enable us to move on to a discussion of the process of professional development planning. In the vocational dynamics framework that has been described, professional development planning is considered one arena of choices that are made on the career continuum; it is an aspect of occupational decision-making. These occupational decisions can be summarized in two broad categories:

Field choices are those which have to do with what occupation to enter, what school to attend for preparatory or *readiness* training, what job to accept, and what roles to assume within the job.

Growth choices are those which relate to decisions about which skills to develop; which values to accept, strengthen, or act out, or change; what knowledge to acquire; which interests to fulfill; which needs to satisfy; and what characteristics to strengthen, change, or "dampen." (The term "dampen" refers to the process which must be sometimes followed when an individual has a characteristic that is inhibiting or detrimental to best functioning, but which is of such a nature that it cannot be completely removed from the personality. Sometimes psychologists speak of "binding" such characteristics, or a complex of them.) Professional development planning involves the application of the compromise theory to growth choices as well as to field choices. What follows is a series of steps to be taken in the process of making growth choices according to this approach.

THE PROCESS OF
PROFESSIONAL DEVELOPMENT PLANNING

Self-Appraisal Discovery, Organization, and Analysis

Most professional persons know more about themselves than they realize but lack a way to distinguish one piece of self-knowledge from another, and many are often unable to incorporate that knowledge clearly in making decisions about personal and professional growth. Recognizing again that lines between the factor sets do not represent dynamic divisions in actual life functioning, it is helpful to begin a self-appraisal by preparing a "self-structure" chart similar to chart 2.

Chart 2

Joseph Churchsmith's Self-Structure[11]

Abilities	Knowledge	Values	Interests	Needs/ Drives	Character- istics
High I.Q. Avg. crea- tivity Strong in: Analysis Coordina- tion Organizing Speaking Weak in: Research Dev. of ideas Supervision	Spanish English Bible Church hist. Political science	Committed to Family Church Com- munity	Speaking Religious activities Music Art Adventure	Authority Status Indepen- dence Social service	Warm Non- assertive Tender- minded Group- dependent Practical Conscien- tious

Done carefully, a real self-structure chart will be much more extensive than Joseph Churchsmith's. Some persons find it helpful to draw it on a large piece of newsprint. In even as oversimplified a portrayal as this one, however, the necessity for compromise to clarify conflicts and take advantage of complementarities is obvious. The strong abilities and interests are complementary, but one of the weak abilities (supervision) may inhibit one of the drives (for authority), as might three of the characteristics (nonassertiveness, tender-mindedness, group dependency). No knowledge of organizations or of sociology is indicated, both of which may be essential in fulfilling the needs for authority and social service and in helping keep the group-dependency factor from being an inhibitor instead of a strength. A few minutes' play with the various conflicts and complementarities in the chart and with ideas about various developmental experiences that might be necessary for the fulfillment of any particular compromise will reveal the potential utility of such a chart for one's own purposes.

Following are some brief suggestions on how an individual might gather such data about himself or herself.[12]

Discovery of Abilities

The functional abilities one uses and finds a purpose in using can be discovered, or clarified, by analyzing in detail the procedures one has followed in acting out *significant processes* (such as marriage, educational ventures, family development, as well as ongoing professional responsibilities such as "ministry in general"), *significant achievements* (different from processes in that goals were accomplished or tasks completed, e.g., "developed a new training program for church officers," or "counseled successfully with a couple who were in great marital distress") and *significant failures* ("something you did not succeed in doing to your own satisfaction" but which was "of greater than usual importance to you—in terms of how it changed your life or what you learned from it").[13] "Such an approach assumes that meaning derives from procedure as often as from result, in fact perhaps more often, and that much dissatisfaction in ministry derives from the production of excellent results through the use of abilities which in themselves have no meaning for the user."[14]

Having organized one's life history according to the categories suggested, one then studies the processes, achievements, and failures listed to see which abilities were used in them, noting which abilities were used (a) *well and with meaning, (b) well but without meaning, (c) poorly but with meaning,* and *(d) poorly and without meaning.* This gives clues to the abilities one finds satisfaction in using, those which are "can do" but do not provide satisfaction, and those which provide satisfaction but are weak. Generally, focusing just on ability development alone, it is wisest to plan to use and develop those abilities which fall into categories a and c, with thought also given to the possibility that further development may add meaning to those in category b, and to the probability that those in category d should be avoided. Thus, in transferring ability lists to the self-structure chart, the most significant terms from categories a and c are always listed, those in category b sometimes, those in d hardly ever.

Ability terminology should be as discrete as possible. Terms defined in the *Dictionary of Occupational Titles* published by the United States Department of Labor are most helpful in this regard. A list developed for use in church career centers uses these terms: observe, research, analyze, develop ideas, write, coordinate, compute, classify, file, copy, mentor, counsel, teach-instruct, supervise, manage, negotiate, organize, persuade/influence, speak, perform, design, build, artistically present, finance, purchase, operate, inspect, maintain, repair, collect.[15]

Description of Knowledge

The section on knowledge is completed by listing all the areas in which one feels competent about the concepts involved. Courses taken, independent study done, learnings through practice, are all guidelines to this section of the self-structure chart (assuming evaluation, of course, to distinguish between that which was merely taken as a course and that which is knowledge). The purpose of this part of the chart is to input and call attention to mastery of concepts, principles, and technical data.

Clarification of Values

It might be more helpful to consider the process involved in clarifying values as "commitments clarification." In so many ways the whole struggle over intentionality, and the purpose, implicit as well as explicit, of examining all the other categories (abilities, interests, knowledge, needs, and characteristics), is to try and clarify values—the total perspective values of life: one's ultimate goals and search for meaning[16] and how one proceeds in moving toward those goals, in searching out meaning. Charlotte Buhler has summarized the complexity of that task in relation to values in a very helpful way.[17]

For growth choice decision-making it is important to simplify the values question in terms of consciously felt commitments, in order to be able to state as clearly as possible, first, the commitments one has made and, second, what commitments may need to be made in order to make possible an integrative compromise essential to intentionality as expressed in profession.

As already mentioned elsewhere[18] such commitments can be thought of in terms of those made to *persons* (Christ, parents, spouse, children, friends), to *concepts* (love, justice, peace), to *organizations and institutions* (church, school, government), and to *groups of persons* (the congregation, the lonely, the sick, the poor). They can also be commitments to roles or positions or occupations which are ideologically weighted (ministry, social work, teaching), or to goals which are reflections of needs in the personality (money, power, affiliation).

Because the whole area of values overlaps so much with everything else, and hence is so diffuse, there are no instruments or tests available which can be used with confidence in a process of clarification. Thus, to state felt commitments in such a way that they can be compared with the other factors is the important task. If commitments are so unclear and confused that they cannot be stated with any certainty, that in itself should be stated, for it points to an area for development.

Joseph Churchsmith describes himself as committed to family, church, and community. Another person may list "serving others," "working for peace," and "achieving intimacy," while a third might list "God," "Christ," "the church" and "the ministry."

The important thing is to struggle with the question of dynamic commitments—those which require action, utilize energy, and influence behavior—as consciously felt "judgment guides."

Discovering Interests

Interests represent attraction to various activities. The *Strong Vocational Interest Blank,* which may be taken at testing centers, provides the most comprehensive way of discovering yours, but you might simply write down those activities of greatest interest to you, choosing from a listing such as this: public speaking, law and politics, business management, sales, merchandising, office practices, military activities, technical supervision, mathematics, science, mechanical, nature, agriculture, adventure, recreational leadership, medical service, social service, religious activities, teaching, music, art, writing.[19]

Specifying Needs for Occupational Satisfaction

Research has shown that there are twenty needs which are particularly important for occupational satisfaction and that each person has a different hierarchy with respect to them. To the extent that an occupation—either the work tasks and environment, or educational training tasks in connection with professional development—provides opportunity for the hierarchy to be satisfied, the satisfaction deriving from professional endeavors will reinforce the individual. The *Minnesota Importance Questionnaire*[20] enables one to discover one's hierarchy through a computerized process that presents needs in these terms: ability utilization, achievement, activity, advancement, authority, company policies, compensation, co-workers, creativity, independence, moral values, recognition, responsibility, security, social service, social status, supervision–human relations, supervision–technical, variety, and working conditions. It, as well as other instruments designed to uncover needs that are important to work satisfaction, can be taken at a counseling center, or one can simply process one's own out in several ways: analyze the lists of life experiences developed for the ability analysis to see what they say about needs and their satisfaction. Which needs and drives were satisfied in the processes, achievements, and failures that were outlined? Which needs seemed to make a difference to the degree of importance attached to a particular achievement, for instance; which needs are recalled as having been frustrated in achievements or failure that, had they been satisfied, might have made a difference in satisfaction gained?

Pinpointing Characteristics

Characteristics, like the other factors, are often discerned in organized fashion only when one takes a personality test or survey, or participates in group or individual therapy oriented toward giving those involved explicit feedback about personality variables. While such approaches are clearly helpful, there are many other resources for helping with such clarification: specifically, the arrangement of feedback received on a daily basis from family members, colleagues, parishioners, and friends (or enemies!), according to some clear concepts of personality. The most logical system of personality description, and in many ways the easiest to grasp, is that developed by Raymond B. Cattell.[21] Using the factors specified by him one can develop a list of strengths and inhibitors in the personality. Just as in the other factor sets, a test (the 16 PF) which measures Cattell's categories in a scientific way is available through counseling services. Many other tests are also available for this purpose.

I have not attempted to be comprehensive in describing the various ways in which the data relevant to a self-structure chart can be collected. The emphasis rather is on the need to put it together in organized fashion so that the factor sets can be compared with each other. It is, of course, ideal to collect the information in as reliable and objective a way as possible, utilizing available professional help, but it is also important to recognize that professionally administered tests and professional counseling are not the only way to understand oneself.

Once the data begins to take shape in the format suggested, it can be checked out with family, friends, or colleagues and corrected by their input. (It should be pointed out here that extremely defensive persons are not likely to learn much from such checking out; neither are they likely to learn much through a professionally administered program of ability and personality evaluation, though there is a greater chance for defenses to be reduced and openness to occur in that setting than in the less formal settings suggested. Interestingly, highly defensive persons resist positive insight about themselves with almost as much rigidity as they do negative insight.)

Having discovered the data suggested, one then charts it and begins to analyze it for conflicts, complementarities, and development ideas. Contrary to popular opinion, development should not focus only upon weak or problem areas; sometimes it is much more productive to build upon strengths. Looking for indications of potentiality is important at this stage.

In analyzing the chart the objective is to *uncover the integrative compromise possibilities which will clarify and enable intentionality*. One is, at this point, trying to develop an *ideal satisfaction profile* and a variety of ways to fulfill it.

The Importance of Satisfaction

Satisfaction is one side of the effectiveness equation. The other side is *satisfactoriness*. A person may be said to be satisfied with his or her occupational endeavors when those endeavors fulfill an appropriate integrative compromise among the factors affecting satisfaction—abilities, knowledge, values, interests, needs, and personality characteristics—and when that compromise is such that it interrelates in meaningful ways with the other facets of life (as indicated in chart 1). Thus, we must consider the whole of life when working out satisfaction plans concerning occupation. This is often done by considering as part of the *values* question the relative importance of each life area. Even when such consideration is not given to the other life contexts, however, work satisfaction will be a function of the kind of compromise worked through and the degree to which it enhances and enables fulfillment of intention.

It is important, therefore, to begin a test of the satisfaction profile by raising questions about the *field choices* one has made or might potentially make. This is helpful as a freeing experience even if the individual has no desire to consider changing his or her occupation. It is particularly essential to struggle with ambiguity about field choices as a preliminary to focusing upon growth choices.

> A major detriment to growth decisions which will contribute to satisfaction and satisfactoriness is ambiguity about field decisions. Struggling endlessly with the question "What shall I be?" some wander, either literally or in fantasy, through consideration of one option after another: "Maybe I should leave the ministry entirely"; "No, the chaplaincy would be a meaningful ministry for me"; "Then again, I always thought I would like teaching." . . . The wanderings and wonderings of such ambiguity are costly, using energy which could be put into function and development if there were greater confidence about wherein satisfaction is likely to be found. It is difficult, if not impossible, to decide, in a consistent and growth-inducing way, about continuing education which will enhance professional development if there is little or no confidence in *continuing,* and no certainty about what one wants to develop the capacity to profess.[22]

As I said earlier in this chapter, intentionality is a continuing process; Rabbi Martin Siegel's questions, however, are questions of intention about ministry, not essentially questions about alternatives to ministry. One way to consider the problem more clearly is to evaluate whether one is confident of fulfilling *intention within ministry* in some way, or whether it appears that another field choice for fulfilling *intention without ministry* must be made. Unfortunately, for reasons such as guilt induced by social pressure within the church, fear about capacity, and anxiety about family needs, many persons who are professionally involved in the church develop crises of integrity and meaning[23] in an effort to avoid dealing with ambiguity about their field.

If self-appraisal leads to extensive questions about field choice, these should be resolved as far as possible before planning growth choices. It is at this point that many persons find a professional consultation with a vocational counselor helpful, for trying to work through such questions without professional assistance can be an exasperating and highly anxiety-producing task. Therapists and spiritual counselors are also frequently helpful in this regard, though their knowledge of occupational dynamics is often inadequate.[24]

The Need to Consider External Realities, Too

As one analyzes the ideal satisfaction profile and struggles with its implications, one will find oneself naturally thinking, too, of the realities which are external to the self. Some of these are personal: the needs and demands of family members, particularly spouse and children; financial requirements; geographical restructions due to extended family requirements and such. Others are nonpersonal: the realities of the "world of work," the society in which one lives or plans to live.

In particular, the realities that grow out of *satisfactoriness requirements* will begin to come to mind. *Satisfactoriness* has to do with the expectations and demands of the work situation, the expressed or implicit understandings of role and function held by those whom the individual is serving (such as a congregation or individual parishioners), and the credential and function expectations of professional organizations, colleagues, or ecclesiastical structures. Satisfactoriness has to do with the fulfillment of external criteria applied to the practitioner, in regard to effectiveness in the work or service being performed, whereas *satisfaction* refers to the meaning, or pleasure, felt by the practitioner. The *ideal satisfaction profile*, then, when it comes to consideration of either field or growth choices, must be looked at in the context of concern for satisfactoriness as well as satisfaction.

Further, the socioeconomic situation, mobility within the profession, the labor supply and demand factors in the broader culture, and situational idiosyncrasies where one currently lives and works, all must be taken into account if field choice considerations are being pondered and, with the exception of those that are outside the ministry, as growth choices are being considered. For instance, labor and supply factors are generally important only if one is considering another field or position, and situational idiosyncrasies are less important if one knows that one will soon be leaving one's current position. A good deal of effort must be given to collecting and analyzing this reality data.

> Any occupation, job, position or role can be described in terms of the abilities essential to it, the interests it might fulfill, the values implicit and explicit in it, and the characteristics it might require, tolerate and not tolerate. For each alternative [being considered], including your present profession and/or job, make up a *satisfactoriness profile*. Consultation and information gathering is necessary, of course, as you seek data about situations unfamiliar to you and correction/enhancement of your understanding of the present situation or professional direction. Persons to consult include: spouse, colleagues, board members, personnel specialists, placement officials, persons in jobs you are analyzing, career counselors, denominational executives, et al.[25]

Other chapters in this book provide resources for analyzing the organization in which one works. This is part of the external reality that must be taken into account.

It is essential, then, in arriving at integrative compromise decisions, to consider the requirements of both satisfaction and satisfactoriness. In this chapter greater attention has been given to the satisfaction profile than to the satisfactoriness demands because it is the writer's experience that satisfaction is often neglected in response to either the other-directed forces in the culture or the simplifications of self-sacrificial theology.[26] Professional effectiveness, much less satisfaction for the individual, is not well served by such a distorted emphasis, nor, in the writer's opinion, is religion enhanced when its leaders are encouraged or trained to see life for the most part in terms of response to those whom they lead or serve.

SUMMARY AND RECAPITULATION

What has been said thus far can be summarized in a statement of *principles for actualizing intentionality through self-appraisal and occupational analysis.*

1. Intentionality is not an end goal but a process requiring attention throughout life, particularly by those whose professions require them to assist others in discovering and maintaining intentionality.

2. Intentionality is served through a process of self-appraisal and reality assessment which leads to integrative compromises in the decision-making about one's own intention.

3. Career development is only one aspect of life, part of a vocational dynamic which also includes concern for family life, religious experience and expression, community involvement, leisure time utilization, and friendships.

4. Professional development planning requires a clarification of field choices as well as attention to growth choices.

5. Consultation with others, those who are close, those who are colleagues, those who are professionally trained to assist, is an important part of the decision-making process.

A PLAN FOR ACTION

The sixth principle would be that all this should result in a developmental plan of action for oneself. If the process has been followed carefully and adequate consultation has been engaged in, such a plan will be more rational than otherwise, will therefore be more filled with potential meaning for the person, and will contribute to satisfaction as well as to satisfactoriness. As the individual "recycles" him- or herself through such a process on a regular basis (in a formal though private way, probably at least once a year), he or she will revise the plan for actualizing intentionality and will also work into the picture the personality data relative to life stages, as well as new understandings of *reality givens* and *reality potentials.*

A further word about reality considerations needs to be said. Frequently reality is thought of only in terms of that which *is;* it is also that which *might be.* While some realities cannot be changed, there is always the possibility of creating a new reality—a new role, a new organization, a new position, a new profession even. Fantasy plays an important part here, for in seeking the integrative compromise it is helpful to fantasize about the possibilities before concentrating too heavily on the reality givens. Maintenance of openness about ways to fulfill intentionality, as well as about different expressions of that intention, stimulates creative thinking not only about oneself, but about the church and the world.

These words of Einstein are significantly corrective to a tendency to rationalize too completely about possibility:

> I believe with Schopenhauer that one of the strongest motives that leads men to art and science is escape from everyday life with its painful crudity and hopeless dreariness, from the fetters of one's own ever-shifting desires. A finely tempered nature longs to escape from personal life into the world of objective perception and thought: this desire may be compared with the townsman's irresistible longing to escape from his noisy cramped surroundings into the high mountains, where the eye ranges freely through the still, pure air and fondly traces the restful contours apparently built for eternity.
>
> With this negative motive there goes a positive one. Man tries to make for himself in the fashion that suits him best a simplified and intelligible picture of the world: he then tries to some extent to substitute this cosmos of his for the world of experience, and thus to overcome it. This is what the painter, the poet, the speculative philosopher, and the natural scientist do, each in his own fashion. Each makes this cosmos and its construction the pivot of his emotional life, in order to find in this way the peace and security that he cannot find within the all-too-narrow realm of swirling personal experience. . . .
>
> The supreme task of the physicist is to arrive at those universal elementary laws from which the cosmos can be built by pure deduction. There is no logical path to these laws; *only intuition, resting on sympathetic understanding can lead to them. . . .*[27]

Any analysis should be experienced as open-minded, as yet to be influenced by the Creative Spirit, by that which may seem impossible today; but this is not to deny the need for planning which will enable one tomorrow to view possibilities as well as self in ways that are beyond comprehension today. This is not a plea for wishful thinking, or for "leaving it all up to God" (an approach that does injustice to all that Scripture teaches, and experience confirms, about both God and humans); rather, it is an expression of concern that the suggested processes be used to *open life up* rather than to close it down.

The components of a plan for action, as finally arrived at, are threefold: (1) the areas of knowledge to be developed or expanded, the abilities to be learned or strengthened, and the characteristics to be mobilized, changed, or bound up must be specified as a result of the satisfaction profile and integrative compromise that is developed; (2) experiences, study programs, personal development processes (such as therapy, group work) which are available or which may be created in response to expressed need must be specified; and (3) ways of financing, freeing time, gaining admission, and such, must be planned. All this requires negotiation with family, colleagues (if one is in a developmental relationship to them), and the providers of the potential opportunities.

NOTES

1. Rollo May, *Love and Will* (New York: W.W. Norton & Co., 1969), pp. 223-25.

2. Mel Ziegler, ed., *Amen: The Diary of Rabbi Martin Siegel* (New York: Fawcett World Library, 1971), pp. 239-40.

3. *Ibid.,* pp. 12-13.

4. May, *Love and Will,* pp. 242-45.

5. See Eli S. Ginzberg et al., *Occupational Choice: An Approach to a General Theory* (New York: Columbia University Press, 1951), for research data supporting this compromise theory of occupational decision-making. See also Thomas E. Brown, "Career Counseling for Ministers," *Journal of Pastoral Care,* vol. XXV, no. 1 (March, 1971) pp. 33-40, for a discussion of its application to career counseling with ministers.

6. See Karen Horney, *Neurosis and Human Growth* (New York: W. W. Norton & Co., 1950), pp. 64ff., for a discussion of the "tyranny of the should."

7. See Thomas E. Brown, "Vocational Crises and Occupational Satisfaction Among Ministers," *Princeton Seminary Bulletin,* vol. LXIII, nos. 2 and 3 (December, 1970), pp. 52-62.

8. Eli Ginzberg, "Toward a Theory of Occupational Choice: A Restatement," *Vocational Guidance Quarterly,* vol. 20, no. 3 (March, 1972), p. 172.

9, 10, 11. Thomas E. Brown, *The Seminarian's Vocational Planning Handbook* (Lancaster Pa.: The Center for Professional Development in Ministry, 1973).

12. See Thomas E. Brown, "First Steps," *Christian Ministry,* May, 1974, for a similar and somewhat briefer discussion of this approach.

13. Thomas E. Brown, *Survey of Resources for Development in Ministry* (Lancaster Pa.: The Center for Professional Development in Ministry, 1973).

14. Brown, "First Steps," p. 17.

15. Available from the Center for Professional Development in Ministry, P.O. Box 1529, Lancaster, Pa. 17604.

16. See Viktor E. Frankl, *The Will to Meaning* (New York: New American Library, 1969).

17. See Charlotte Buhler, *Values in Psychotherapy* (Glencoe: The Free Press, 1962).

18. See Brown, "First Steps."

19. *Ibid.* See also David P. Campbell, *Handbook for the Strong Vocational Interest Blank* (Stanford: Stanford University Press, 1971).

20. Fred H. Borgen, David J. Weiss et al., *Occupational Reinforcer Patterns* (Minneapolis: University of Minnesota, Industrial Relations Center, 1968).

21. See Raymond B. Cattell, "Personality Pinned Down," *Psychology Today,* July, 1973, pp. 41-46.

22. Brown, "First Steps."

23. See Brown, "Vocational Crises."

24. Before consulting a commercial counseling agency, read Caroline Donnelly, "A Brief Case Against Executive Job Counselors," *Money*, November, 1973, pp. 81 ff. A list of church-related career centers is available from the Church Career Development Council, 475 Riverside Drive, New York, N.Y. 10027.

25. Brown, "First Steps."

26. See David Roberts, *Psychotherapy and a Christian View of Man* (New York: Charles Scribner's Sons, 1950), for a very helpful discussion of "static" and "dynamic" views of salvation and Christian life.

27. Cited in Banesh Hoffmann and Helen Dukas, *Albert Einstein: Creator and Rebel* (New York: Viking Press, 1972), pp. 221-22. *Italics added*.

Getting a Job

JOHN C. HARRIS

The well-documented and well-publicized surplus of clergy within mainline Protestant denominations has made the search for work a problematic task for nearly all ministers in those traditions. Clergy are not alone in confronting a turbulent, often tight job market. Productive occupations like aerospace engineer and stockbroker can become depressed almost overnight. Recent Bureau of Labor statistics indicate that four out of five people change occupations at least once in their lives. The meaning of such statistics for a particular professional class or group of workers is not always readily apparent. Yet one fact is clear: most of us must cope with a rapidly changing world of work. For ministers, this means learning to adopt new attitudes toward employment and to acquire a new set of job-related abilities—how to search for the right kind of work setting, how to interview effectively, how to negotiate work agreements, and how to remain marketable over a span of years.

A PASSIVE TRADITION

Only in recent years have ministers had to actively seek work. I recall vividly conversations with a nearby

John C. Harris is assistant to the bishop for clergy development of the Episcopal Diocese of Washington.

colleague while I was rector of St. John's Church, Oxon Hill, Maryland. During those years (1958–1965) he and I talked regularly by telephone—sharing news, asking advice, offering encouragement. Every now and then, one of us would cautiously ask the other, "Had any calls?" Tense moments. Invariably when both of us confessed, "No," as we always did except on a few occasions, I felt a mixture of both relief and uneasiness. Relief that he had not received a call while I, like a plain girl at the dance, had been overlooked; uneasiness that perhaps "the system" would not work for me a second time.

More recently he and I have discussed these ex-changes and some of the unwitting assumptions they reveal about the church as an occupational system. For one thing, we assumed we would be ministers for life, and that the church would "somehow" provide us with the right congregation, at least often enough to prevent us from getting stuck in one place. For another, we assumed the bishop was our ally: if worse came to worst, he would be willing and effective in recommending our name to any vacant church we suggested. Third, we unquestioningly accepted two seldom verbalized maxims: (1) never openly advertise your availability, and (2) never approach a vacant church directly on your own. In short, where work and vocation were con-cerned, we operated from a tradition of enforced passivity. In those years there was a part of me that relished that kind of dependence and never dreamed there might be a price to pay. As a result, in me the capacity to search for work remained largely unde-veloped, as it has with many clergy. I planned to work hard, shine brightly, and wait to be found.

The growing surplus of clergy has radically altered the situation. Nowadays, clergy must compete for work in a buyer's market in which churches and judicatories can afford to be highly selective. Church executives are far more aware of their responsibility to recommend to a vacant congregation not just any minister who wants to move, but those whose values and abilities fit that church's needs, problems, and life-style. In point of fact, no "system" exists to move a minister along at the right time, nor to take care of his or her needs for productive, meaningful work. Most judicatory offices and the denominational placement services are primarily organized to serve the needs of the institution, not the needs of individual pastors. In this environment, the minister's new task is to make the shift from a passive to an active mode with respect to his or her vocation and career. In other words, he or she must learn to become self-directing and self-initiating, to take personal responsibility for his or her own development, vocation, and quality of employment. This means, in part, that clergy need to shuck off the old expectation that the church can be counted on to find them work. They need to see the church structures such as bishops' offices and employment services not as caretakers, but as resources they can thoughtfully put to use in their own behalf.

BECOMING ACTIVE:
SOME THINGS TO KEEP IN MIND

1. This intensely competitive environment carries two implications for clergy which are often overlooked. First, to find the right kind of work today, a minister must use a high degree of personal initiative. Second, he or she must be able to develop a strategy for job search based on sound self-knowledge and accurate reading of the placement practice within the judicatories where he or she wants to work.

2. Bart Lloyd, director of the Mid-Atlantic Career Center in Washington, D.C., maintains that many people looking for new work mistakenly think of jobs simply as

slots to be filled, without much informed thought about their own personal requirements. If Lloyd is right, and I believe he is, this means you have to know what you do well, what abilities you enjoy using, what you (and your family) need from your ministry, at this point in your life. The first step, then, is to crystallize your personal and vocational objectives and to understand accurately your abilities and needs.

3. Ministers move into new work by means of personal influence and their ability to use effectively networks of personal connection and communication. In my experience, the critical factor in securing an interview for a job-seeking minister is the personal recommendation of a local pastor or layperson known to the congregation's leadership. Therefore, one basic aim of a search strategy is to uncover such networks and organize them to help you.

4. A second aim of a search strategy is to get interviewed by those with the power to hire—e.g., a congregational board, a church executive. Yet interviews alone are not the point. There are important qualifications. Your basic target is to be interviewed by those with the power to hire you for work that *uses your abilities, in a place pleasing to you and your family, at a salary that is reasonable and appropriate, and under conditions which encourage continuing vocational growth and personal development.* Turning up those kinds of interviews is what takes the time, research, and hard work.

5. Remember, each judicatory has its own unique placement processes and key actors who play influential roles in helping clergy secure interviews with search committees and congregational boards. In some judicatories, for example, church law requires a parish to interview and call only clergy recommended by the judicatory executive and lay-clergy committee. In

others, parishes interview and call clergy without significant contact with church executives. A job search strategy must include a procedure for finding out how individual judicatories handle placement and who the chief players are.

6. As a general practice, search committees and church boards will usually grant interviews on the recommendation of—

—a judicatory official
—canonically authorized committees (as, for example, in the Episcopal Diocese of Delaware)
—a known and respected minister
—a known and respected layperson

7. Each parish church is a unique human community with its special environment, history, life-style, needs, and challenges. A sound job search strategy should permit you to find and explore those congregations whose current goals, problems, and style are reasonably congruent with your strengths, values, and personal needs. The belief that a pastor can serve all churches equally well is a piece of destructive mythology that does not match experience.

DEVELOPING A JOB SEARCH STRATEGY

1. Begin by clarifying your own values, abilities and needs. This can be a thoughtful in-depth process using resources like church-subsidized career centers or a colleague group that has skilled leadership in vocational assessment. Or you can use the kind of self-directed exercises Richard N. Bolles describes in his book, *What Color is Your Parachute?* (New York: Crown Publishers, 1973). Either way you will want to uncover and describe:

—The satisfactions you want from your next parish or position

—The values you want your work and service to express

—Your characteristic leadership style and preferences

—Personal shortcomings that get in the way of your assets

—Special family or personal requirements

Nail down specific aspects such as:

—Where you want to live; where you definitely won't live

—The judicatories in which you want to work (reduce your list to a primary one of no more than four or five)

—Job search objectives—type of position and type of setting

—Types of congregational needs, challenges, and problems that intrigue and excite you (this is a key piece; give it particular attention)

—Salary and other work requirements, e.g., cost of living increases; plan for evaluation

—House: church's? yours? equity plan?

2. Unless you can already count on a number of colleagues who will effectively boost your name for the kind of work you want on a moment's notice, you will need to spend time and energy building your own network of personal influence. As Dick Bolles puts it, "Finding the right job is a job in itself." After you have determined the answers to the questions in the immediately preceding section, the next task has a threefold aim.

You want to—

a. learn how each of your priority judicatories is handling placement (in many areas this is now a rapidly changing picture);

b. develop a tactic for getting regular information on vacancies that reasonably match your criteria;

c. develop contacts that will help you get interviews with people in a position to hire or who can be of special assistance in your search.

An effective method for accomplishing all three is to develop a list of those executives, clergy, and laity whom you know and whom you feel could be helpful to you. (In particular, concentrate on your preferred geographic areas.) Ask them the following questions:

—What is the executive's role? Does he have special policies about placement?

—Are there any rules covering clergy placement?

—Is there a vacancy consultation procedure?

—Who is in charge?

—What do you recommend I do to increase my chances of finding the right work for me?

—Can I call you once a month and get filled in on what is open?

—(If in doubt): How willing would you be to recommend my name if I asked you? Very? Moderately? Slightly?

—What is the prevailing norm in your area about approaching a church calling committee directly and asking for an interview?

4. Keep your personnel profile up to date. Some executives won't recommend a minister without a profile, and calling committees are using denominational placement services with increasing frequency to put together their primary candidate list. Revise your profile approximately every eighteen months, and allow extra time for its processing.

5. Sit down with your own judicatory leader. Take the plunge and find out the extent of his interest in recommending you to churches within his jurisdiction, just what type of church he sees you as fitted for, what he sees to be your special strengths. Ask him (but only if you can stand to hear it) how he would describe your "flat sides" to a parish. Finally, ask him if there is anything he

needs from you in order to support you in his jurisdiction or to recommend you to others.

6. Learn to spot job search resources in your area. In my diocese, part of my job is to help clergy develop job search strategies, prepare for interviews, write good résumés, and so on. Seminary placement offices can be excellent resources. In some regions, judicatory staff have formed active communications networks among themselves to help clergy find work.

7. Develop a concise, one-page résumé which highlights your job objectives, special abilities, accomplishments and gains in your present position, education and training, special requirements for your work in the future, and a series of brief phrases which convey glimpses into your life and self. Richard Lathrop's *Who's Hiring Who?* (Washington, D.C.: Human Resources Press, 1971) is an excellent resource for résumé writers.

Scattering résumés shotgun fashion is seldom worth the postage. Résumés are necessary information pieces for a church executive and/or search committee who want to interview you. People with considerable job search experience say emphatically that the letter which accompanies the résumé is just as important as the résumé and sometimes more so.

8. Unless you are an old hand at the job search, the interview is another area for serious research. You may want to explore the services of the career center in your region. For example, the Mid-Atlantic Career Center in Washington has several excellent reading references for interviewing for work in the church, plus a lot of sound advice to give. During the past year, I have been asked on four occasions to help men think through an upcoming job interview—anticipating difficulties, planning what to cover, looking at the process, then debriefing afterwards. Other people are an important resource in helping you prepare for interviewing.

9. In preparing for an interview, it is extremely important to do your homework well. Study thoroughly all materials sent you by the congregation. Read with an eye toward identifying their needs. Concentrate on discovering where there are overlaps between their needs and critical problems and your own abilities and preferences. What you are looking for is work that calls for your particular abilities and arouses your enthusiasm. What a congregation or organization looks for is someone whose values and talents suit its particular needs.

TWO ADDITIONAL COMMENTS

1. The best time to search for your next job is when you don't have to. Crisis and panic looking are obvious enemies to doing a careful exploration for the right work setting for you. A sense of anticipation helps. In particular, that means accurate knowledge of your own changing needs and sufficient knowledge of your present organization to know when conditions warrant a search for new work.

2. In searching for the right kind of work, your position is strongest when you don't have to have the job for which you are interviewing. Thus, time is a central factor. You must allow enough time to search without feeling that sort of grinding urgency that pushes people to take "anything they can get."

Under today's conditions, finding the right work for you takes a long time. Give yourself nine months, preferably a year. *To repeat:* Getting the right job is a job in itself. For most of us, it requires time, research, specific strategies, a tolerance for disappointment, and the stamina of a long-distance runner.

A Lifelong Process of Learning

CONNOLLY C. GAMBLE, JR.

In this chapter I want to build on the theme that Tom Brown developed at the beginning of this section. Now that you have gone through the steps he outlined, how do you go about developing a lifelong process of learning that expresses your intentions? My purpose is to think with you about what continuing education involves, why it is important, and how to get the help you need to make it a creative part of your life.

CONTINUING EDUCATION FOR MINISTRY

What comes to your mind as you hear the words "continuing education"? Perhaps you think of a short-term event to which someone goes—usually away from home—for some days of intensive study. I think that picture is too limited. Its popularity warns us that we need mutual understanding of "continuing education" if our meanings are to meet.

After years of careful thought Mark Rouch has worked out this definition: continuing education is "an individual's personally designed learning program which begins when basic formal education ends and continues

Connolly C. Gamble, Jr., is executive secretary of the Society for the Advancement of Continuing Education for Ministry and director of continuing education at Union Theological Seminary in Richmond, Virginia.

throughout a career and beyond. An unfolding process, it links together personal study and reflection and participation in organized group events."[1]

Notice how Rouch's definition picks up the importance of *intention:* you work out your own design rather than passively adopting what someone else has conceived. And its *length:* a process across a person's career, not a project finished in a few years' time. And its *flexibility:* it has a place for both individual and group involvements in study. I hope you will reflect on Rouch's description for a while.

My own definition is a simple one which I offer for your thinking: Continuing education is *systematic, sustained study.* Each of these words is important, I believe. Continuing education involves *study*—really digging to uncover the roots of a subject, then examining them carefully and thinking about relations and meanings. It involves a *system,* put together as an orderly and coherent program across a career, with stages worked out so that one goal or process grows out of its predecessor and builds cumulatively on it. I agree with Rouch that the system belongs to you—the learner—not to those agencies or schools that sponsor events and offer continuing education services. The pattern of study components is your property, not to be handed over to someone else to manage. And continuing education is a *sustained* process, not an achievement that you can check off as "finished"! As you design it, you may put together some units leading to an academic degree—but the process goes on past the earning of any and all degrees. With only a few breathers you keep your program going as long as you are actively engaged in ministry (which may be years past your retirement date!).

Look again at the definition I have offered you: continuing education involves your systematic, sustained study. Your sources are unrestricted: you can vary the focus and means of your continuing education, using books, magazines, newspapers, conferences, interviews, classes, workshops, cassettes, a guided bus tour, television, radio, film, telephone. You are not limited in your goals and content. You can study informally as well as in formal ways.

While my definition is wide-ranging, it does not include everything in the universe! It stresses *your* study, *your organized* study, *your sustained, systematic* study! That may eliminate some of those brief encounters in which for a day or two you are exposed to the essence of someone's study, yet you are not involved in the quest through your own initiative and effort. That stress may exclude signing up for an event just because you happened to receive an ad about it, or because your neighbor wants to go and would like company on the trip. That emphasis may require a rethinking of your priorities so that you are willing to commit yourself to a specific educational effort in order to attain some valued knowledge and/or skills. It means you will carry through with this project because you believe it has important payoff for you!

WHY YOU NEED TO CONTINUE YOUR EDUCATION

If you have stayed with me in this chapter, you may now be asking yourself, "Why is it important for me to give myself to systematic, sustained study? What makes it worthwhile?" Let me try to share some reasons.

One is the need to *supplement* what we learned in school. Those courses provide the foundation, but only that—no matter how far we advanced in them. Every subject field is changing continuously. If you value keeping up to date on the field you began to explore in school, you have to study continually.

Think back to your school years. You were limited in what you could work into the curricula of those few years. No matter how broad your choices, you had to pick some from among the options. That forced selection meant that some courses and subjects had to wait until a later stage in your career—after you entered the ministry.

You need to continue your education for a second reason: to *initiate* learning in response to new problems and changed situations. The rapid changes in society and in ourselves press us with new learning needs. No one could anticipate in a formal curriculum all the complex effects of technology and the new problems it has generated. For example, the complicated ethical questions opened up by genetic manipulation, organ transplants, and artificial extension of life could not have been faced in a curriculum in the 1950s. The changing forms of life in inner cities, on large university campuses, in high-rise apartments, and in sparsely populated rural areas require us to develop new concepts of church, evangelism, and ministry. Through continuing education we can formulate new approaches to meet new problems and opportunities.

Third, you need to continue your education as a means of *personal development*. Continuing education affects you as a person, as well as what you are learning. You need an overhaul that puts your learning into new modules and relations. You need to reconstruct your earlier learning which may now be outmoded by changing situations. This can have two important results. Often the retooling generates new patterns and fresh content; interdisciplinary approaches have given people new insights and understandings. Also, the overhaul can have a powerful personal result: it can help you to discover or recover a sense of wholeness.

You can see that I have moved onto the border that continuing education shares with therapy. You need to continue your education because you must weigh the ambiguities and ferment that life in ministry inevitably involves. You need to build into your life opportunities to think out meanings of life, drawing on those resources that your faith-heritage provides in its various strands and reweaving a pattern of integrity.

INCENTIVES TO CONTINUE YOUR EDUCATION

You may be responding to my argument thus far, "Those are theoretic needs for continuing education—but I am more interested in knowing why *I* should continue my education." So I want to share some of the reasons for you to consider.

One motive is the desire to be more competent. When you take on a new job or a new responsibility, you may expect to prepare specifically for that work. Increasingly church employers are recognizing the need for special training if people are to work effectively, and so are providing time and money for continuing education to make specialized study possible.

But I am thinking also of the person who plans to stay in the same occupation and wants to grow in mastery of that position. As I talk with people about continuing education, I find they have an increasing concern for developing a keener edge on various elements of the job. And I get some reports that, as a person gets more competent, he or she finds that new approaches and skills bring new meaning and qualities to the job.

I know some persons who are impelled by a different motive: they are looking for self-fulfillment. They want to propel life forward, to grow, to make progress, and to achieve instead of stagnate. Sometimes that desire is hard to express in words. You develop a feeling that some areas of knowledge and certain skills may be launching pads to project you into richer living, and so you want to learn in order to enrich life.

A third motive seems closely related: you just want to understand some subject better! Some express this as curiosity—wanting to know more about things. Some call it the will to be informed. You may be like the explorer who is constantly pressing on into unknown lands: the more you see, the more you want to see and know in ever sharper detail.

Still another motive probes the inner being: the need to rethink priorities in your life. Do you find that some stages of your career are marked by restlessness and uncertainty about the future? At times like those this motive takes on special importance: the desire to have time for reflecting about possibilities in life. The chance to do this may bring new perspectives which help you discover and plan for refocused goals in your personal life and in your professional ministry.

A fifth motive for pursuing adult education often ranks high. You want to move out of your isolation and into an attractive setting with change of pace and new associations. Familiar settings seem to breed a hunger for stimulation. "Everywhere I go, I run into the same people" is the way some express their feeling. We may be stifled by the feeling that we are cut off from creative people. We seek new ventures in continuing education with the hope that fresh breezes may blow into our stale lives with the discovery of kindred spirits.

Closely allied to this motive is another that may prompt your continuing education—the desire to escape parish frustrations for a time. Professionals (physicians, lawyers, teachers, pastors) express this need often: to be released briefly from the pressure of phones and appointment books. Even though continuing education programs may be available in the immediate area, some of our colleagues go away from home for residential events in order to shake free of local entanglements.

You may have noticed that I have not yet mentioned a widely felt reason for continuing education—the promise of higher status. Some want the enhanced prestige attached to education. In a society that affirms educational achievement it is natural that we should value progress in learning especially when publicity accompanies the accomplishment of goals like earning a degree or receiving appointment to a leadership position.

What prompts your interest in continuing education? It may be one or more of these incentives—or perhaps you have other reasons that push or pull you. On a scale of values some may be more appropriate than others. My chief concern is getting started learning on a systematic, sustained basis—and part of what you learn may be better reasons for your education than the ones you started out with!

BARRIERS THAT MAY IMPEDE
YOUR CONTINUING EDUCATION

You may find it helpful to look honestly at some of the things that seem to block continuing education. If you can appraise the kinds of resistance that must be overcome, and stake out the hostile territory, you may be able to make more progress!

Here is one obstacle that I observe: some persons do not understand the importance of continuing education. Some think education is "completed" in youth and see no point to adult leaning programs. Some are harsh judges of the minister when he shows interest in study: they think he is a recluse who prefers to escape from contact with people into his ivory tower. Some resent intellectual achievement and consider it undesirable and unworthy: "A person ought to get to work on important things." In contemporary culture there is an anti-intellectual strain that breeds distrust of the "egghead."

This low opinion of study is not confined to the laity. Some of our peers in the clergy award study a low priority. In some communities there develops among churchmen an atmosphere that is unfavorable toward continuing education. Daniel Walker observed that if you invite a minister to a meeting and he has a committee meeting or wedding or funeral, his refusal is understood and accepted. But if he refuses by saying, "I'm sorry, I can't come to the meeting; I bought a fine book yesterday and will stay home and read it," he'll be considered "uncooperative, an intellectual snob, or just odd."[2]

You may have felt a second obstacle to continuing education: the minister does not always have ready-made opportunities to share the results of study. One of my colleagues is convinced that peer group participation is essential to a minister's continuing education. He has developed an extensive program to enable groups of ministers and laity to work together in guided study courses. Groups form by entering into a learning contract, so that each member finds that commitments made to partners in learning make it easier to keep a high priority for personal study.[3]

You can build in your own incentives to study as a priority through the engagements and responsibilities you accept. By your own choice you can support your intention to engage in continuing education, cultivating speaking dates or preaching/teaching opportunities that will then press you to engage in specific study as preparation.

Honesty compels us to acknowledge another obstacle to continuing education: it is hard to maintain a disciplined life. "Life's fundamental discipline is to know where you are going," Daniel Walker says. Discipline and order are not the same. As a minister at the call of parishioners you may find it very difficult to lead an ordered existence, but you can still impose discipline on the disorder of your days. "The way a man orders his life is an individual matter, and may not be of too much importance. But the way he disciplines his life is of profound importance," Walker insists.[4]

You may find that an answer to this problem is to study every day you are at home base, regardless of how you feel or what other commitments are included in that day. Arnold Toynbee described his method as a historian: "I write every morning, whether I am in the mood or not." Forty-five minutes a day devoted to a study project across a six-day working week adds up in a working year (eleven months) to 12,960 minutes—more than two hundred hours at your disposal if the intention is there day by day!

Friedrich von Hügel observed that a living faith is a continual holding together of three separate and unfriendly—often hostile—elements: the institutional, the intellectual, and the mystical. If any one is exalted at the expense of the others, if any one is given free rein, some perversion of the faith occurs: a tradition-bound observance of the rules of the institution, or a sterile rationalism, or an excessive emotionalism. How can we keep in appropriate tension these three unfriendly loyalties—to the institution, to our intellectual growth, and to God? If we do not, wandering prophets who need to be loyal to their vision will be lost to the church. If we do not, we will have housekeepers of an institution caught in a race for promotion and rewards and successes. If we do not, we will have scholars withdrawn from the rat race but still giving some kind of respectability to the institution.[5]

You may have been waiting for this fourth deterrent to continuing education—the problem of time and money! Some are reluctant to ask for time off (with salary maintained) and funds from their parishioners, because they do not want to seem self-seeking. Some are already underpaid and cannot afford funds for conference tuition and residence costs except by squeezing their own families. In 1968 the National Council of Churches' study of clergy incomes found that 71 percent of Protestant ministers had no time allotment for continuing education as a part of their working contracts; and 78 percent received no money for continuing education from their parishes.

In the last three years the situation has improved. The United Methodist Church has designated funds in its Ministerial Education Fund that may be used for continuing education of ministers. Presbyteries of the United Presbyterian and Presbyterian, U.S., churches have increasingly required continuing education time and money to be included in parish calls of ministers. Some Episcopal dioceses have raised large sums for endowment, or set apart money from sale of property, for continuing education of clergy. The Lutheran Church in America has developed PACE—Pastors' Aid in Continuing Education—with a congregation and pastor each contributing to an account in his or her name, designated for continuing education. The United Church of Canada requires its ministers to spend three weeks annually in continuing education, and provides a yearly budget of $200,000 for this purpose. Thus in various ways the church bodies are recognizing the importance of continuing education and encouraging if not requiring time and money for it as a condition of clergy employment.

Still another obstacle you may have anticipated: the church as a system offers little incentive to your continuing education. I am reminded of a New Yorker cartoon showing two men chained by their wrists to massive wall bolts above their heads. Huge shackles fasten their ankles to the base of the wall. Their bodies sag, listless and slack, against the damp stone of the dungeon. Their clothes are disheveled, their faces bearded, their eyes glassy. High overhead one window opens to the world, and a single shaft of light penetrates the gloom. One of the men has twisted his head toward his companion spread-eagled on the wall, and is saying, "Now, here's my plan!"

The planning of a career in ministry has hardly existed until recent years. Most churches have required certain preparatory steps into the ordained ministry, but between that event and retirement is "chaos, neglect, accident, and too often, tragedy."[6] With the increasing problem of placement or assignment in a number of denominations, the panic to find opportunity for pastoral moves becomes ever more threatening. How many hundreds—or thousands—of clergy are caught up in a terrifying private struggle for career advancement?

One response to this complex circumstance is the Academy of Parish Clergy, a nationwide society of Protestant, Roman Catholic, and Jewish religious leaders who have banded together to provide legitimate peer rewards for continuing education and progress toward competence in ministry. Through peer group support in evaluating performance and collective judgments as to the needed professional skills, they are trying to form a new image of effective parish leadership by competent professionals. They are seeking to influence denominations and seminaries to reform personnel practices and educational programs. You may take a major step forward by joining the academy if you feel otherwise unsupported by your church system in your educational efforts.

You may also find constructive help at a career development center. A career counselor in a regional ecumenical agency can help you to assess your needs where you are ministering, and at various stages of your life. The counselor can act as your adviser, support, coordinator, and colleague. I know a good number of ministers who regard their two and a half days at a career center as a turning point in their lives, a time when they began to perceive more accurately their strengths and limits.

For some ministers a sixth block to continuing education is the memory of a painful seminary career now seen as largely irrelevant. The fear that continuing education will turn out to be "more of the same" has deterred some, especially when they have thought about taking part in events sponsored by seminaries.

As a seminary professor I urge you to recognize that many seminaries are changing and ought not to be stereotyped as you remember them from ten or twenty years ago. You have some reasons for optimism in the emerging curricula that view theological education as a career-long process for every minister. Some leaders are reforming the whole system so that learning appropriate to seminary is provided there and learning best provided *after* seminary can be provided at that time.

Aware of the diversity and tensions that mark congregations, seminaries are seeing the necessity of including management, communication, and organizational development skills—sometimes for seminarians, more often for post-seminary learning. Perhaps more important, seminaries are offering new models of learning: teaching seminarians how to learn by choosing types, models, ways of approach to systematic study in a sector. Increasingly the professor is stressing his most valuable contribution: helping the student to learn how to learn in that field, developing skill in asking crucial questions, gaining skill in internalizing meanings as a learner.

Some seminaries are responding to a viewpoint expressed by John Gardner:

> If we indoctrinate the young person in an elaborate set of fixed beliefs, we are insuring his early obsolescence. The alternative is to develop skills, attitudes, habits of mind

and the kind of knowledge and understanding that will be the instruments of continuous change and growth on the part of the young person. Then we will have fashioned a system that provides for its own continuous renewal. ... All too often we are giving our young people cut flowers when we should be teaching them to grow their own plants. ... Education can lay a broad and firm base for a lifetime of learning and growth. The individual who begins with such a broad base will always have some capacity to function as a generalist, no matter how deeply he chooses to specialize. Education at its best will develop the individual's inner resources to the point where he can learn (and will *want* to learn) on his own. It will equip him to cope with unforeseen challenges and to survive as a versatile individual in an unpredictable world.[7]

Seminary alumni and faculty and seminarians need to work together candidly to reform seminary education, to develop these qualities in every theological school, both in the basic curriculum and in the seminary's program of continuing education.

Continuing education at a seminary is important, I believe, not only because it enables faculty to share their theories and concepts with parish ministers, but also because it allows pastors to interpret their experience in ministry to those teaching in seminary: "This is how we find it!" I think a good many of the progressive developments in seminaries during the past several years can be traced to the steady influence that parish ministers have had on seminary faculty when the pastors have gone to campuses for continuing education programs.

MAKING A START IN YOUR CONTINUING EDUCATION

My aim in this section is to offer some practical suggestions to help you get started in your continuing education.

115

1. As a pastor you can set goals for your ministry, growing out of the objectives developed for and by the parish where you are at work. You can press your congregation for responsible decisions that will link them with you in mutual action. Together you can establish plans for changes that are going to be sought in people and groups and structures.

2. When you reach some clarity about your goals—immediate and longer-range—you can begin to settle your priorities in education by placing these parish-oriented goals alongside your personal/professional learning needs. A good way to assess these latter is to use a checklist of pastoral competences. The Academy of Parish Clergy has identified some twenty skills as basic to "competence in the ministry." Union Theological Seminary in Virginia has developed a list of seventy-seven competences that can be used as a standard for assessing knowledge and skills in ministry. You may find it a turning point in your career to use such an evaluative standard with an honest friend—layperson or minister!

3. After you have assessed your learning needs (what you should be, know, and be able to do), you can then think through the resources for continuing education to meet those needs.

Here I would strongly emphasize one point: basic to any program of continuing education is study at home using your personal library, resources you can borrow from friends and libraries nearby, and loans by mail from university and seminary libraries. Until you have made your plans for learning at home, with clearly defined study objectives to be achieved at your own desk, you have no clear criteria for selecting events and learning units elsewhere. No other locale offers the learning potential to be found in your home setting, *if* you exploit the resources that can be assembled for work at home.

Guided study programs developed by some

seminaries can help you with two major problems: selection of materials and access to these materials. The Guided Study Programs available from Union Theological Seminary in Virginia and Louisville Presbyterian Theological Seminary offer guides on more than a hundred subjects, prepared by experts in these areas and listing a manageable number of titles—fifteen, ordinarily. The recommended materials can then be borrowed from these two seminary libraries by mail from anywhere in the United States. This kind of program may help you to tailor a coherent plan for your cumulative learning at home. With your home study plans established, you have regular input for your normal tasks. You can then look forward to occasional study at other centers to provide concentrated learning opportunities designed to supplement your home study program.[8]

4. With some ideas about learning needs and educational resources, you can talk with lay people in your congregation, especially the officers, to define and refine the emerging program of learning. Lay people who understand why the pastor gives a high priority to study can explain to other church members that your learning is your oxygen tube sustaining a vital ministry to and with the laity. You program will then represent a compromise or adjustment, taking account of your personal desires and interests and the church members' assessment of what you need to learn in order to be most effective as their minister.

5. Across your career as a pastor you should try to space some opportunities for more extended study leave. Some denominations now encourage these sabbatical leaves. The prospect of a study period may well offset the fatigue and drain that beset some careers. With interim pastors now widely available, your congregation can thrive while you are on leave for six to twelve months!

HELPING TO CHANGE THE SYSTEM

The steps suggested up to this point have dealt primarily with the minister in relation to the congregation. There is another part of the system that we must consider: the personnel system of the denomination. Many of the morale problems of ministers are rooted in the inefficient personnel systems found in many churches. Whatever influence or weight you have or can develop ought to be put into the effort to change the structure.

In many denominations a focal problem is placement: the movement of ministers from one parish to another when they wish or need to move. In recent years pastoral changes have slowed in most communions, as fewer new churches have been organized and more ministers have been available to serve as pastors. Movement of pastors among parishes has been a primary way to introduce change into churches and ministers. When that movement slows down, so does the rate of change! If you value change in the church and its leadership, you must help find workable approaches.

One essential is a personnel system that incorporates all ordained ministers of the denomination and links all the agencies that enlist, educate, deploy, and support them as annuitants. The aim should be the most effective use of the talents of every minister in the entire denomination. Where feasible, the denomination should link with other church bodies so that ministers could move across lines to serve in other communions.

Essential also is reorganization of many inadequate congregations to form viable, creative centers for worship and work, financially able to support a full-time pastor and a dynamic program, and with sufficient lay membership to engage in vibrant congregational ministry. Indicators point to a parish of at least 250 communicants as possessing the strength to launch and sustain a mission to the world in that fashion.

Thus, I am stressing three changes needed in the church: a more adequate personnel system and place-ment opportunities; parish development in viable units; and the minister as a growing person. Without the first two changes, the third is trapped: systems may crush very competent persons. As a churchman I am aware that all three changes are priority agenda at all levels of the church's life—the congregation, the regional judicatory, and the entire denomination.

With the hope and expectation that you will help to make these corporate changes I conclude this chapter with this urgent plea: that you take responsibility for your life under God, deciding on your aims and pushing steadily toward your career goals, and drawing upon continuing education as a resource to achieve these purposes in ministry.

NOTES

1. Mark A. Rouch, *Competent Ministry: A Guide to Effective Continuing Education* (Nashville: Abingdon Press, 1974), p.16.

2. Daniel D. Walker, *The Human Problems of the Minister* (New York: Harper & Brothers, 1960), p. 53.

3. For information on this group study program by mail, write to Dr. Richard T. Murray, Director of Continuing Education, Perkins School of Theology, Dallas, Texas 75222.

4. Walker, *Human Problems of the Minister,* p. 127.

5. I am indebted to Brewer Burnett for this observation from Friedrich von Hügel's *The Mystical Element in Religion.*

6. Clement Welsh, *Concepts in Continuing Education for Ministry* (Position paper from the Executive Council of the Episcopal Church, New York, 1968).

7. John W. Gardner, *Self-Renewal* (New York: Harper & Row, 1965), pp. 21, 26.

8. See my article, "Short-Term Programs of Continuing Education," in James B. Hofrenning, ed., *The Continuing Quest: Opportunities, Resources, and Programs in Post-Seminary Education* (Minneapolis: Augsburg Publishing House, 1970), pp. 67-74.

PART III

THE INTENTIONAL CONGREGATION

Intentional ministers help bring intentional and vital congregations into being. The facilitating link between the two is, of course, negotiation. The first chapter in this section reviews the ways goal-setting and evaluation enable the congregation to be clearer and more effective about the role of its minister or ministers. The second chapter is a helpful and concise summary of intentionality and negotiation in church organization development.

Goal-Setting and Evaluation

JAMES GUNN

Where there is no vision the people perish.
Proverbs 19:18

God's people have always been sustained by a vision of the incomparable love of God. In any particular moment of history the task of the church is to translate that vision of God's love into specific, concrete individual and corporate actions. Without the vision the reconciling actions cease, or become merely church activities, a going through of motions for motions' sake. The image of the minister as the intentional leader of the congregation is formed out of a concern for the crucial role played by the minister in relation to the vision that informs the church's actions and without which the people perish.

The most prominent characteristic of the intentional minister is vision. The most important skill of the intentional minister is effectiveness in negotiating that vision with officers and congregation so that everything the congregation does and experiences is informed by that vision. The intentional minister is characterized by a passionate purposefulness and a significant degree of effectiveness in sharing that passion with the congregation and involving the congregation in the achievement of that purpose.

James Gunn is executive director of Professional Church Leadership for the National Council of Churches.

Another way to talk about this dimension of the intentional minister is to use the word "spirit," the controlling, overriding thrust of one's life in which the vision that grasps us is revealed. The controlling, overriding thrust of Jesus' life, his spirit, discloses the vision of the love of God that was the basis of his intentionality. To speak of intentionality in ministry is to ask, What kind of spirit, what kind of controlling, overriding thrust animates our ministry, and what vision does it disclose?

The intentional minister, we maintain, sets goals and has some reliable ways and regular occasions to evaluate effectiveness both in communicating those goals and in achieving them. Goal-setting has to do with translating vision into a specific description of a desired state of affairs. Evaluation has to do with enhancing and improving one's effectiveness with a congregation in negotiating and achieving those goals. Goal-setting and evaluation are among the important negotiation skills of the intentional minister.

In more specific and perhaps more existential terms, goal-setting and evaluation have to do with the minister's own soul-searching questions about success, achievement, and satisfaction in ministry over the years. The younger minister just a few years beyond ordination has one notion of success. The minister in middle years now well established in a career in ministry probably has a different notion of success. But in our time both ministers are less and less sure of what constitutes significant achievement or success in ministry. An increasingly pluralistic society and denominational system robs today's minister of the kinds of social consensus on success in ministry that were possible in less pluralistic times. If, as it is asserted, religion is becoming more and more a private affair in the midst of a cultural emphasis on "doing your own thing," it is increasingly difficult for the minister to have socially supported norms for success or achievement. Goal-setting and evaluation have emerged in our day as means by which the minister can attack this problem head on instead of continuing to drift toward the retirement years with a kind of free-floating anxiety about whether or not his or her ministry will in the end add up to anything that can be called "success" or "solid achievement."

Much of the research on the contemporary ministry has focused on the conflicting or diffuse expectations of the minister on the part of congregations, denominational leaders, the community, and society in general. Many ministers are not sure what they are good for, what they ought to be about, or what constitutes a faithful and effective ministry. When a particular theological understanding of mission or a particular strategy for the congregation's involvement in mission becomes fashionable, many ministers have encountered debilitating conflict and unmanageable stress. Being unintentional about one's ministry has become for many an unconscious coping style or survival technique. The resulting damage to morale and personal integrity has been immense.

Seen against this background, goal-setting and evaluation are skills which, properly used, hold some promise of helping the minister regain a sense of purpose and integrity. As practical skills they have been appropriated from the social sciences, particularly the growing research on organizational behavior and the technologies of organizational development that have emerged out of such research. In the next chapter, G. Douglass Lewis deals specifically with church organizational development as one of the negotiation skills of the intentional minister. The minister's personal and professional goal-setting and evaluation cannot and should not be separated from his or her continuing involvement in congregational goal-setting and evaluation. But for purposes of exploration and discussion the focus of this chapter is upon goal-setting and evaluation from the point of view of the minister's own ministry as if it could be separated from the church's ministry. In the course of our discussion we will examine the crucial interrelationship between the minister's ministry and the church's ministry.

GOAL-SETTING AND EVALUATION: MORE THAN A RATIONAL PROCESS

Acknowledging goal-setting and evaluation as concepts and techniques appropriated from the behavioral sciences should not be taken as a negative judgment, but it should remind us that goal-setting and evaluation in the context of the behavioral sciences are based upon an essentially rational view of human organizations and presuppose the rational management of individual and corporate life. It is important that we see the intentional minister as the rational manager of a volunteer organization, but if we understand intentionality only in these terms we fail to do justice to all the a-rational and nonrational dimensions of existence that also contribute to our image of the intentional minister. Those of us who constituted the working team for this volume struggled very early in our discussion with whether or not the concept of intentionality might inadvertently be taken to exclude the symbolic character of ministry, the characteristics of intuition and spontaneity, and the quality of simply being God's person among and with God's people. It was our feeling that intentionality as a master concept did in fact include the intentionality of the dancer or painter, the intentionality of the gambler or the adventurer, and the intentionality of the mystic or contemplative. But we did recognize the predisposition of our Western consciousness to freight intentionality with more rationality than we intend. Part of the difficulty is that the rational dimensions of the concept of the intentional minister lend themselves more readily to rational exploration and the printed page than do the intuitive symbolic and creative dimensions of intentionality. It is, after all, easier to write a how-to manual on goal-setting and evaluation than on painting, dancing, or creative imagining!

DISCOVERING GOALS THROUGH EVALUATION

The growing literature makes it clear that goal-setting and evaluation are two phases of a single continuous process in which the intentional minister is always engaged. Meaningful goals are more often *discovered* out of the experience of evaluation than designed out of thin air. If we were to diagram the process, it might look something like this:

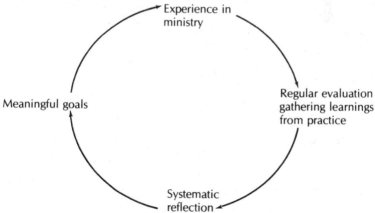

As we work to achieve certain goals we discover how really meaningful they are, how effective we are in achieving them, how realistic we were in setting them, and how appropriate they are in our particular social context. We begin to form judgments about our goals as a basis for reshaping them.

Much of this continuing process is quite unconscious. The intentional minister, we maintain, is consciously deliberate in his efforts to keep this process going and to be specific and clear about both goals and accomplishments in relation to them. In the absence of such conscious and deliberate maintenance of the goal-setting and evaluation process many ministers experience a vague, free-floating anxiety about themselves and their ministry and plague themselves with unexamined guilt feelings about their competence and relevance as leaders of the congregation.

KEEPING IN TOUCH WITH FEELINGS

What does the minister bring to this continuous process of goal discovery and evaluation, and what can he or she do to enhance the process?

In the first place we each bring a bundle of very personal feelings about ourselves and our practice of ministry. We bring both current feelings and a history of feelings. Regardless of the general character of those feelings, it is important that we get in touch with what we are really feeling about ourselves and our ministry and share those feelings with someone with whom there is a relationship of trust and caring—a wife or husband, a colleague or friend. There is no possible way to discover meaningful goals if we have repressed our real feelings about ourselves and our ministry. Without honesty about feelings the minister will continue to set phony (and impossible) goals until he or she finally gives up having any goals at all.

The human potential movement growing out of humanistic psychology has helped us rediscover the importance of acknowledging our real feelings and of finding appropriate ways to express our feelings to others. Many ministers in recent years have benefited from personal growth, improved human relations, and improved communication skills through laboratory training programs offered by a wide variety of church and non-church agencies. A number of trainers have developed a specific life planning workshop design for couples that facilitates the process of identifying feelings, values, and life goals in a setting where the sharing of such personal data with spouses and trusted colleagues is enhanced.

These group work designs emerging out of the laboratory learning and the human potential movement have not been without their critics who point to either the demonic character of behavior based solely on feelings or the unreal character of "instant" community which many designs seem to foster. Other critics would point to the fallacious presuppositions regarding human goodness and perfectability explicit in much of the human potential movement. My purpose here is not to respond to these critics but to underscore the importance of getting in touch with one's real feelings and staying in touch as a necessary part of the intentional minister's goal-setting and evaluation. We in the church are particularly prone to repress our negative feelings, which results in distrusting and repressing all our feelings. The goals we set for ourselves and our ministry when we are out of touch with our real feelings become for us a new legalistic and tyrannical obligation impossible to achieve, and the suggestion that we evaluate ourselves in relation to such goals becomes an unbearable threat to the delicate system of merely coping that constitutes our operational integrity. We need to stay in touch with our feelings and to utilize the various resources available to us for discovering and trusting our feelings.

FEEDBACK

Feelings dominate our lives and motivate our work far more than most of us are willing to acknowledge. The minister who continually feels underpaid, underrecognized, undervalued, or misperceived by the congregation is obviously already doing a whole lot of unconscious evaluation in relation to a bunch of (probably) unarticulated goals. In most instances such a minister is probably doing a great deal of "mind reading" regarding the perceptions, expectations, and feelings of the congregation or of colleagues and judicatory leaders. In getting in touch with and dealing with one's feelings it is important to have some kind of reliable feedback, some kind of opportunity to check out what others really think and feel. The object is to minimize the amount of "mind reading" we are doing about ourselves and our ministry.

Some ministers have developed a simple survey sheet which they distribute to the congregation from time to time, inviting a response to questions about different aspects of the minister's role, such as preaching, leading worship, counseling, visiting, community leadership. This kind of information gathering can be significantly enhanced if the minister asks several of the congregation's leaders to be consultants in working out the instrument, legitimating its use by the congregation, and assessing the results. Such consultants can also provide personal support to the minister in working on whatever goals have emerged out of the congregation's feedback. An outside consultant—a colleague or personal friend, not a member of the congregation—can also be a helpful resource in getting feedback from the congregation. The important point is that the intentional minister will have some regular and reliable means for eliciting useful feedback from the congregation so as to minimize the amount of "mind reading" he or she is doing with respect to the congregation's perceptions, evaluation, and feelings.

VALUES AND COMPETENCIES
IN RELATION TO ROLE EXPECTATIONS

The minister also brings to the goal-setting and evaluation process a unique assortment of skills and competencies and a personal history of the employment of those skills and competencies in some kind of socially supported work setting. Many ministers are unaware of the diversity and the quality of the skills and experience they bring to their ministry at any particular moment or in any particular setting in their career. Goal-setting and evaluation can be done effectively only when it is based on a realistic self-knowledge of one's professional strengths and assets and one's personal values and preferences. It is self-defeating to set professional goals that have no relationship to what one does well and enjoys doing, and it is obvious that any evaluation of such goals would be a form of self-punishment.

The intentional minister sets goals and evaluates out of some realistic awareness of what he or she does well and enjoys doing. Over a period of time most of us develop some "educated hunches," if not dogmatic convictions, about what we do best and where our major satisfactions are found; but the ministry demands generalists, and we may be involved in such a diversity of activities that we lose a clear focus on ourselves, particularly if in our ministry we are trying to respond to diverse and conflicting congregational expectations. In that situation we may need a more systematic effort to identify our competencies and satisfactions.

Church career assessment and counseling has emerged in recent years in response to the minister's need to be clear about about personal characteristics and professional competencies in developing meaning-ful career goals and in utilizing the continuing education opportunities currently available to help him or her achieve those goals. In part 2 of this volume Thomas Brown, dealt with the process developed in the church career counseling centers which religious leaders can use in building greater personal clarity about abilities, skills, interests, values, and preferences. A self-administered process has been designed for the Lutheran Church in America by George Garver and is currently being field tested. In addition to these resources there are occupational/vocational testing and counseling services available in most communities through universities or colleges, state agencies, or private testing and counsel-ing services.

Whichever resource the minister utilizes in gaining greater self-knowledge about competencies and satisfac-tions, the important point is that many ministers have found a new freedom to be far more intentional about their ministry because they are setting personal and professional goals that have some relationship to who they really are.

The goal-setting and evaluation process of the inten-tional minister also includes another component in addition to being in touch with one's real feelings and a knowledge of one's competencies and preferences. As mentioned earlier, the minister's goal-setting and evalua-tion cannot be separated from the congregation's goals and its evaluation of its life and work in relation to those goals. Ideally, at least, the goals of the intentional minister are discovered in large measure in relation to the goals of the intentional congregation. The assump-tion is that the minister's sense of passion and purpose is in direct proportion to the congregation's clarity about the meaning and purpose of its corporate life. In some instances a minister's effectiveness may be judged by how well he or she maintains a personal vision of the transforming power of the love of God in the face of a seemingly apathetic congregation, but even Jonah was forced to come to terms with the effectiveness of his preaching in the face of his personal preference for failure! The congregation that has a visible and communicable sense of what it is about will "produce" ministerial leadership characterized by purposefulness and a sense of professional worth.

The reader may refer to Douglass Lewis's chapter on church organizational development, keeping in mind that the intentional minister is not simply a passive process-enabler as the congregation develops goals but actively negotiates for goals that represent the best possible fit with personal strengths, commitments, and satisfactions. Here again it is apparent that the minister must work from as strong a position of self-knowledge as possible and trust the importance and significance of his or her personal feelings.

The goals of the intentional minister will not be exhausted by or coterminous with the congregation's goals, but there will at least be a meaningful degree of congruence. Nor will the skills and competencies needed by the congregation to achieve its goals be only the skills and competencies of the ministerial leadership. The evaluation of the congregation's life and work, by the same token, will be more than just an evaluation of the minister's performance; but the evaluation of the minister, when done within the context of the congregation's evaluation, takes on the dimensions of teamwork and mutual trust and accountability. It begins to destroy the image of the minister as the sole and lonely performer whose performance is paid for by the spectators and is judged only for its entertainment value.

SUMMARY

To the goal-discovery and evaluation process the intentional minister brings an awareness of personal feelings, a measure of self-knowledge with respect to competencies and preferences, and an internalization of the congregation's goals in which the minister has negotiated his or her own vision and role expectation.

It should be obvious by now that goal-setting and evaluation carry with them an implicit valuation of change in the church. The intentional minister needs to be realistic about both the congregation's interest in change and his or her own personal interest in and commitment to change.

Church Organizational Development

G. DOUGLASS LEWIS

"Organizational development" is one of those new "in" terms being used in the church today. Some people have visions of it as the latest way to save the church. Others are quite hazy about what it means and what it does but are eager to get on the bandwagon. Still others, convinced that it is merely a new set of gimmicks and is not theoretically or theologically sound, are skeptical. The truth is, as usual, somewhere in the middle. As a discipline emerging out of the behavioral sciences, organization development offers for the church valuable new technology. It will perhaps be even more useful as church people develop and adapt its theory and practice more fully. The purpose of this chapter is to discuss two concepts of organizational development: "intentionality" and "negotiation." The chapter will also show how these two concepts can be embodied in the life of the church through two processes called "self-assessment" and "goal-setting."

Persons by their very nature are intentional and project their intentions in the form of goals, things they want to accomplish. In other words, goals are the concrete expressions of persons' intentions. But, because a person lives in a society in which other people have differing intentions and goals, he or she must learn

G. Douglass Lewis is coordinator of Parish Development for the Hartford Seminary Foundation, Hartford, Connecticut.

to work out or negotiate these differences so that all parties can achieve some of their goals. Organizations, then, are the concrete and necessary embodiment of the intentions and goals of persons who make up their membership. In fact, persons living within social structures have very little way of expressing their intentions or working on their goals other than through the variety of organizations of which they are a part. These social units may vary all the way from the family to schools to government to businesses to churches. But they are all instruments of the intentionality of those who seek to fulfill their goals through them.

Some ways are more effective than others for organizations to structure and run themselves in order that the persons within them and the organization itself may achieve their goals. The field of church organization development is an attempt to understand what processes enable this to happen and thus to promote health and effectiveness in churches.

EMERGENCE OF ORGANIZATIONAL DEVELOPMENT

Organizational development (O.D.) has evolved as a field or discipline since World War II. Obviously, persons have been trying to develop organizations since man began living in societies. Most of these efforts, called "management" or "leadership," were aimed at controlling the organization and those persons within it in order to achieve the goals the managers or leaders determined. Unlike management control, O.D. is based on a new understanding of persons which comes from psychology (particularly personality theory), sociology, organizational and systems theory, and group dynamics, and it takes seriously what the individual person's goals are. This new understanding of persons includes their motives for action, how they function in organizational settings, and how organizations have their own dynamics which affect persons within them—new knowledge which is of significant assistance to those working within organizations. They can now base their intentions and actions on known patterns and dynamics that explain individual, group, and organizational behavior. This ability to explain, predict, and reorder makes it more likely that those within the particular social setting can fulfill their own intentions.

The operating definition of O.D. that is assumed in this chapter is: organization development is a series of planned efforts, primarily educative, training, and consultative in nature, which are designed to change the norms, structures, processes, and behaviors of the organization itself and the people within it in order to accomplish more effectively the goals of the organization and the goals of the persons within it. A basic assumption of O.D. is that an organization will more likely tap the main sources of motivation and energy of its constituents for work toward the organization's goals if it also pays attention to the needs and goals of those constituents. Thus, O.D. tries to free and enable individuals first to identify and then to find ways to pursue their hopes, intentions, and goals. One way of doing this is to help those in control become more aware of and sensitive to the constituents' needs and goals. The attempt to achieve a balance between individual needs and the organization's goals leads directly to the concepts of intentionality and negotiation.

THEORY OF INTENTIONALITY AND NEGOTIATION

Intentionality (what I want to do) and negotiation (how can we agree together on what we will do?) are two concepts that are not widely used in the church. Obligation (what I ought to do) and control (how can I determine what you will do?) are often more dominant themes. It has been more difficult for the church to acknowledge the legitimacy of intentionality than to develop a means (negotiation) by which the variety of individual goals can determine larger church goals.

There are several reasons for this difficulty. Some clergy see their primary role as priest, pastor, and prophet rather than the seemingly mundane job of administrator, organizer, and planner. By focusing on the prophetic or priestly role, they often reinforce obligation (what others ought to be doing) and thus attempt to control the behavior of others. They do not understand that stressing obligations alone will inevitably lead to dissatisfaction, rebellion, and other forms of resistance. These may include lack of attendance, decreased financial giving, or finally even withdrawal.

Most ministers have not learned to think about the church as an organization or to take seriously the pluralistic set of intentions and goals present among their constituency. Consequently, they have not developed the knowledge and skills necessary to institute processes within their churches which can lead to healthy and creative goal negotiation. They often do not realize that church organizations, and the work of managing them, aren't necessary evils or additional burdens but a real opportunity for ministry.

Clergy often ignore the fact that intentionality (what one wants to do) is always present as a motivating factor in behavior. Since organizational matters provide the arena in which "intentionality" is expressed and "negotiations" take place, the pastor who spends a minimal amount of time and energy as a manager soon discovers that it is difficult to accomplish his or her goals or to know what others' goals are. The temptation is to resort to various forms of manipulation in order to retain control and to ensure that his or her goals are fulfilled.

The minister's problem is even greater than that of managers in other types of organizations because the church is by nature voluntary. A minister cannot command obedience like a prison warden in his coercive organization, nor can he pay persons to do certain things as a businessman does in utilitarian organizations. A church with its voluntary constituency discovers that its membership can easily disappear or offer various forms of resistance (no show, no pay) when the church is not moving in a direction they desire.

Types of Goals

A pluralistic and competing set of intentions and goals is always operative within the life of an organization. One way to look at this fact is to recognize three types of goals that are always operating in any church organization. (1) There are *personal* goals, which each individual brings, and which may or may not have implications for the church but will determine some of that individual's behavior. An example would be a person sitting in a worship service Sunday morning whose primary goal for the day is to get on the golf course. Consequently, he will be thinking about getting out of the church service early and rushing to the golf course more than he will be paying attention to the minister's sermon. (2) Each individual has *personal goals for the organization.* That is, each person who invests enough of himself or herself in belonging to the church has some things he or she wants it to do, and he or she will express these goals in a variety of ways. For example, a person who has children in the church school program might be very eager for the church to concentrate many of its resources there instead of in programs outside the church building. Another person, who is highly committed to involving the church in social action programs in the community, will be opposed to spending more money on the physical plant and internal program of the church. (3) The *organization* always has *goals.* These may be derived from its history and tradition, or they may be commonly agreed-upon directions by large or small groups. In either case they determine the programs and expenditures of the church. An example might be the church that has always had a paid choir. Few questions are ever raised at budget-planning time about the money spent on the choir. Other programs, in fact, are cut to support the choir. Any person raising questions or suggesting that other programs might have priority meets with resistance and maybe even hostility.

Private and Public Negotiations

Many church organizations have operated on the assumption that the intentions and goals of people, including the leader, must be kept private and not made public. The negotiations as to which intentions will become dominant and which will determine the church's goals are carried out in a private manner. When most of the information and processes are private it is easier for persons to be manipulated. Even when the intention of the leaders is not to manipulate, the uncertainty on the part of those who have little information leads them to suspect that they are being controlled by others. Once these suspicions get started there are very few ways to clear them up through private processes. When suspicions and assumptions go un- checked and not validated, a basic mistrust grows. The cycle is extended when those who feel that they are outside the channels of information in decision-making aren't able to know what is happening or to influence what is happening. Since people are not getting an adequate hearing, they either withdraw their commit- ment and support from the church or become more aggressive and hostile in attempting to block other people's goals. The cycle continues to escalate when the leadership reacts defensively to this withdrawal or hostility by becoming more private and manipulative or attempts to exercise a tighter control on the dissidents.

In contrast to private styles of operating, a public style of leadership is committed to open negotiation between differing goals. With public negotiation, it is less possible to manipulate other persons because each person's intentions and goals are made known. Open negotiations are less likely to create mistrust or to allow false assumptions to float around unexamined. As a result there is less likelihood that people will feel that their points of view are not being heard and that they have no influence on what is happening. As this cycle escalates, the person whose intentions and goals are influencing the direction of the organization is more likely to increase his or her commitment and involvement.

PROCESSES FOR
INTENTIONALITY AND NEGOTIATION

How one develops ways of negotiating the different intentions and goals of persons within a church can be illustrated by looking at two different processes that, when carried on publicly rather than privately, can move the organization toward health and effectiveness. These two processes are self-assessment and goal-setting.

Self-Assessment

Self-assessment is a process through which persons and organizations look at themselves, where they are, and where they would like to be. Self-assessment means something different from diagnosis, which is a process common to most O.D. efforts. In diagnosis an outside consultant comes in, gathers data from a variety of sources, and then feeds it back to those in responsible positions. They then decide what course of action is to be taken in relation to the data.

Self-assessment is similar to diagnosis, but it stresses developing a process whereby those within the organization do their own data-gathering, interpret the meaning of it, and plan their own course of action. This approach is particularly important in a voluntary organization such as the church. Persons within a voluntary organization are under less compulsion to act on any data about themselves which someone from the outside gives or feeds back to them than are those in a utilitarian organization such as a business, or a coercive organization such as a prison. Those within a voluntary organization can easily withdraw their time, energy, and commitment when confronted by data which from their perspective is uncomfortable or demands some undesirable action on their part. Consequently, if self-assessment is to have any change effect, those who are to be affected by the data should be involved in dealing with it from the initial collection to the final action.

Self-assessment should also be public rather than private. It must be a process which allows persons to share openly with each other their perceptions of what is happening and what should be happening. If this process remains private, there is never any common data base from which persons can negotiate a joint decision about the actions they will take or the directions they will move in. Public self-assessment, then, is a process of generating valid data, i.e., persons' perceptions and feelings, about what is happening and what they wish would happen.

Good self-assessment should always lead to some action, new behavior or affirmation of old behaviors, based on the information gathered. Good self-assessment is never static. It builds a growthful dynamic into the life of an organization.

We and the organizations of which we are a part do not always have the capacity to deal with the true data about ourselves. That capacity must be carefully and steadily built. The building of that capacity is one of the key renewing processes in the life of an organization. It is not a process that can be commanded or instituted suddenly, but one which must be developed. The development, I am suggesting, begins through the processes of self-assessment.

The following examples illustrate how self-assessment can be done in churches. A key committee in a local church had lost its vitality. Starting at eight, its meetings dragged on until midnight. There were endless debates over trivia. Members left grumbling to themselves that it was just another typical church meeting. Attendance declined until there was always less than a quorum. The chairperson finally requested the pastor to admonish and "motivate" the members to be more faithful in their duty to the church and the committee.

The pastor responded by suggesting that they build some simple self-assessment procedures into the life of the committee. They began simply by spending ten minutes at the end of each meeting asking two questions: What did you like and find helpful about this meeting? What could have made it better and more helpful? At first they merely wrote the verbal responses of committee members on newsprint. After a couple of meetings some members suggested that they redesign the meeting along the lines of the suggestions that came during the self-assessment.

As the committee became more accustomed to this process they developed more precise methods for self-assessment, finally selecting a set of categories: How did we use our time? Was my input heard by other members? Did we accomplish our tasks for the meeting? How did we make decisions? In each category they assessed how they had performed and what they might do next time to improve. Slowly committee members began to realize that they could change the way they were operating. The meetings did change. They grew shorter, but more was accomplished. Members began to feel more responsibility for what they were accomplishing. Attendance began to increase. This change did not occur overnight, but it did occur as the committee developed the capacity to assess itself and its performance, and then to change to meet members' goals for it.

The new dynamic and energy that became available to the committee from its members stemmed from the fact that their thoughts, feelings, perceptions, and intentions could now be made public and could thus affect the life and direction of that committee. Once these various feelings, perceptions, and intentions became public the members determined the direction and work of the committee. No longer could the chairperson or pastor control the direction. Neither were they burdened with having to carry this responsibility alone.

A larger-scale example of self-assessment was initiated by a congregation of about five hundred members. They had a small leadership group that was carrying most of the work in the church, with general apathy reigning among a majority of the members. They began by requesting that all those attending worship services on a particular Sunday morning fill out a self-assessment instrument designed to generate some feedback of the feelings, perceptions, and hopes of the members about their congregation. The instrument consisted of a series of statements such as: I feel the congregation is able to cope with change; I feel that conflict/disagreements are adequately dealt with; I feel we have an adequate stewardship program; I feel we have an adequate education program; and others designed to cover various aspects of the congregation's life. Under each question there was a 1–7 scale between dissatisfied and satisfied so that each person could mark how relatively satisfied or dissatisfied he or she was about that area of the congregation's life and program.

Later in the week about sixty persons met to assess the data. A large chart was put up showing the number of responses to each question and how the marks were spread on the continuum between satisfied and dissatisfied. The group focused on those areas which had a large number on the dissatisfied side. Task forces were set up to explore what might be done in these areas. In every case the task forces were in large part made up of persons who had expressed dissatisfaction in that area. The question they continually addressed to themselves and other members of the congregation was: What would have to happen in this area for me to move from the dissatisfied to the satisfied end of the scale?

The task forces began meeting on the same night of the week, and at the end of their meetings they would share with each other what they were doing. In this way, the momentum and work from one group tended to affect and encourage the others. Gradually the task forces expanded to include other persons who had also expressed dissatisfaction in their area, and, more important, they continued to gather data from the congregation about members' feelings, hopes, and intentions in this area. The response to this input shaped the committees' work. It took almost two years for the whole congregation to feel the effects of the work begun by the first self-assessment, but by involving more and more members in the process, new vitality and a sense of new direction and new style emerged for that congregation.

Goal-Setting

The second process by which intentions and goals are negotiated within organizations and which, when conducted publicly, can lead to health is goal-setting. An operating definition of goal-setting is that it is a process whereby the variety of intentions of persons within an organization can be expressed in concrete goals and then means are designed which can lead to the achievement of these goals. Behind this definition is also a set of assumptions which informs the goal-setting process.

The first assumption is that persons are intentional, goal-directed beings. They have needs, drives, wishes, and hopes which get expressed in some kind of goal toward which their behavior is directed. Their behavior is always intentional. That is, a certain behavior is designed to do or accomplish something that is important to the person. This does not mean that all behavior is well thought out or planned or that persons are even cognitively aware of the goal toward which their striving is directed. It does mean that persons are not unintending pawns of a causal chain of prior events. Personal behavior, though affected by prior events, present circumstances, and an anticipated future, always has an intentional element within it. It is this intentionality which is the heart of a goal-setting process.

The best way to understand persons and an organization is through their goals. Persons often have a very difficult time explaining why they did a particular thing. Many times they even have trouble explaining what they are trying to accomplish through a particular action. However, it is easier, and in the long run more useful, to help them clarify what they are trying to accomplish (what goal they are moving toward) rather than to explain why they acted in a certain way. One of the functions of a goal-setting process is to enable an

146

institution and the individuals within it to clarify what they intend or want to do and to move toward that goal.

Since the primary motivation of a person is directed toward working on his or her goals, organizations which are alive and healthy are those in which a large number of the organization's goals and the members' goals for the organization are either synonymous or very close together. The fact that a person has primary energy for his or her own goals does not mean he or she is totally self-centered and unconcerned about other persons: one of the most important goals might be to help others work on their goals. It does mean that persons are not very motivated to work on goals that really belong to someone else and are imposed on them as an "ought" or obligation. Many churches discover this the hard way. By imposing upon their members goals which do not match the members' goals, they suddenly discover that there is no human energy or motivation available to work on these goals. This lack of motivation can express itself in a variety of ways. People promise to do something but do not get around to it. They raise what seem to be irrelevant objections. They do not give money. They may even stop attending or leave altogether.

In some cases persons within the church discover that the formal organization, the official church structure, tends to block them in accomplishing their goals. As a result, they develop an informal system which enables them to circumvent the formal organization and achieve their goals. In some churches most of the energy goes into these informal systems. They become very private in nature, one informal system competing with another and with the formal organization as well. The effect is to make the formal organization ineffective and to shut off the main channel of input for most persons in the church.

An example can be found in the way major program and budget decisions get made in some churches. The formal organization usually has committees in program areas which are supposed to be in touch with and involve those whose needs the program serves. All the committees then bring a recommendation to a central coordinating board, the church council, so that each program is weighed on its merits alongside other programs and in light of the major goals and priorities of the church. What usually happens, however, is quite different. The pastor and a small group of lay people decide what the goal priorities are to be and then privately decide which programs will be pushed and which will not. In many cases these decisions get communicated to the program committees before they present their ideas to the council. Only those ideas that would be approved anyway are presented. As a result, most lay people feel that the church is basically unconcerned about their needs and goals and that, in the final analysis, they have no way of helping to determine the goals of their church.

Public goal-setting, whether it is done within a small group or within a total congregation, is designed to create a setting and a process through which all members of the organization can make their intentions known, their goals explicit, and can influence the direction of that church organization. Once such a process begins to work, new energy begins to flow in the system, because persons will put their energy and commitment where they have an opportunity to work on their goals.

Why does this not happen more often in church organizations? There are several reasons. First, to open up the process and make it public means that some individuals, including the pastor, may lose some of their power to make the key decisions and determine the goals of the church. Second, when such a process is working, it tends to change the organization. It may demand new structures or arrangements in order to achieve a new set of goals. It may change the roles that some persons play, including the pastor's. It may develop new norms about what is acceptable and nonacceptable behavior within the church. Finally, it may create conflict or allow conflict to be made public, as the competing goals are negotiated.

All these changes are genuinely threatening and consequently are usually resisted. But, to be alive, to have a membership that is involved, active, and committed, a church must have some means whereby persons can make known their intentions, identify their goals, and have the opportunity to develop the program, structures, and organizational arrangements they need in order to work for the accomplishment of these goals. When these opportunities and means do not exist, there will be apathy and lack of involvement and commitment.

There are a variety of methods for carrying out a public goal-setting process within a congregation. One church wanted to involve as many of its members as possible. The leaders began by inviting every member to a small group meeting in someone's home to initiate gathering data on members' intentions and goals. Other churches have used their existing committee structure to gather data from those members interested mainly in a particular area. Again, the technology (how to do it) can vary and is not as important as the principle. The healthy church organization is the one which constantly works at developing at every level of its life public processes whereby persons can make known their intentions and goals and can work on their fulfillment within that organization.

I hope it is obvious by now that self-assessment and goal-setting are closely linked. In fact, it is difficult to do one without the other. Both are absolutely essential for making known the intentions and goals of persons within organizations. They also provide ways in which these differing intentions can be negotiated to determine a direction for a church that will command the energy, involvement, and commitment of the largest number of its constituents. Goal-setting and self-assessment are the life-giving processes of an organization. Without them a church tends to stagnate, become apathetic, and even die.

PART IV

SMALL ISSUES AND MASSIVE REVELATION

"Small" issues such as money, family, and leisure can reveal the urgent need for more intentionality and better negotiation as much as career planning and congregation development. In this chapter Bob Kemper, from his experience as a pastor, and editor of Christian Ministry *magazine, presents sharp and fresh challenges for intentionality and negotiation throughout the whole of the minister's life.*

Small Issues and Massive Revelation

ROBERT G. KEMPER

Clergy are neither hopeless nor helpless. They are no longer the proverbial cork dashed about by a sea of tempestuous forces. Clergy already have helpful resources within their own hands and others within their grasp if they will intentionally employ what they have and extend themselves to acquire what they want. This is no less true of the smaller issues and experiences of their professional and private lives than it is of the larger, more formidable issues others have addressed in this volume.

This chapter aims to set forth a series of advocacies about these smaller issues. These are not the make-or-break issues, the cutting edge shaping a new tomorrow. Rather, they are the bits and pieces of ministerial existence which, taken collectively, comprise a pattern, a life-style, a self-image. For the most part these pastoral trivia are unexamined and unchallenged and, for that reason, unyielding. They have a self-perpetuating inertia which is frightening. In a time of shaking foundations these rafters are too secure.

My central advocacy is deceptively simple: gird up your loins like human beings and stand. Be responsible for yourself, your profession, your life-style. Such an

Robert G. Kemper is editor of *Christian Ministry* and pastor of the United Church of Christ, Western Springs, Illinois.

advocacy is another face of intentionality and negotiation. This face is accusatory and assertive. It accuses the clergy of allowing detrimental patterns of life and work to develop through inaction. It calls on those clergy to be responsible about their self-interests. Intentionality, I will argue, extends to a host of mundane matters which previously have been untended, allowing the tares to choke the pastoral wheat.

Consider a few examples of minor matters which when looked at as intentional advocacies are revelatory of one's self- and professional interests.

First, *clergy ought to be paid more money.* Clergy are programmed to believe that "the love of money is the root of evil." In the wake of that simple aphorism gross injustices are done. It distorts certain elemental insights of psychology and theology, and is outrageous economics! The authors of the creation myth in Genesis go to great lengths to affirm the goodness of material creation. They do not assert a superiority of the spiritual over the material. Even if one does wish to assert the primacy of the spirit over the material, the vows of poverty and not just low wages are more appropriate. A curious fact of low wages is that they increase the power of materialism; i.e., a shoestring income virtually requires one to adopt a mind-set which measures everything one does in terms of its economic implications. That measurement is prima facie evidence of rampant materialism. If liberation from material concerns is the objective, the low-wage syndrome has the opposite effect.

But there are other, more fundamental insights about clergy salaries to set forth. Much of the contemporary American Protestant ethos was conceived in a rural, agrarian society; clergy salaries emerged from that ethos and go unchallenged in a society that is dramatically different from its origins. In that earlier, agrarian society salaries were geared to subsistence levels. That was acceptable then because the *real* pay of clergy was psychic compensation. That is, one received the rewards one needed and desired as a formidable community leader, the best-educated man in town, who was, along with several others, the "power structure" of small-town America. One does not quibble about the size of the monthly paycheck if one is a wealthy person in the vaults of one's own psyche.

A second unexamined factor of today's salary scale for clergy is that the society has changed its concept of what money is and does. While clergy were being nourished on the "root of evil" maxim, society was maturing to learn that money is a symbol of love and esteem—as well as a source of things malevolent. Money is what you invest in, that which you admire and desire. It has become the token of affirmation to persons, institutions, commodities, and life-styles. Corporate executives, for example, revel in their year-end bonus. Are they base, crass, materialistic souls? Yes, just like the rest of us. But they understand something else about that bonus, which clergy have yet to examine. In today's world a boss finds it hard to say to a valued employee, "Harry, you are a good man, you do good work, I need you, I love you for what you are and what you do." Instead, he says, "Harry, here's your bonus." (Or, "Sorry, Harry, but we can't give you a bonus this year.") The communication takes place. The symbol of money makes Harry feel valued and productive. One can cite a lengthy list of societal aberrations, from defense spending to pornography, to show that money is an extension of a people's true values.

Another, more embarrassing factor is the "take" system which clergy salaries generate. Clergy can become dignified chiselers. They will ask for discounts on retail purchases; they will find doctors and dentists who "look favorably upon fellow practitioners of the healing arts." In my work with a philanthropic publishing firm I discovered that one dared not pass on rising costs to one's clergy subscribers lest an increase in price cause them to cancel their subscriptions because of their economic deprivation. Sorry, but I find this corner-cutting, or, to call it by its right name, chiseling, morally repugnant and professionally debilitating.

These three observations about this small issue of salary point to a more massive revelation, viz., that low clergy salaries are rooted in low self-esteem. My advocacy is not really a dollar-and-cents issue; rather, it is an issue of self-perception and the ways in which others perceive the role and status of the clergy. It is by no means certain that raising the salary of clergy—say to the level of some worthy vocation in our society, like that of a movie star—would substantially alter the performance of clergy. But I do think being intentional about one's salary should represent a freedom from a veneer of piety which glosses over many economic injustices.

Intentionality about one's own salary has a larger context. Clergy tend to be naïve, uninformed, and sometimes downright irresponsible about a cluster of economic issues. Partly because of misplaced piety and partly because of their own salary situation, clergy have tended to shy away from money matters. Seminaries do not consider economics fit for theological curricula; the denomination does little to increase clergy sophistication in these matters. Among clergy the whole scope of economic issues in their personal finances—insurance, housing, investments, etc.—is in disarray. But even worse, the clergy's missionary zeal for religious institutions is considerably undermined by their reluctance to lead in the financial concerns of those institutions. No doubt the prevailing views among clergy about stewardship—their own and those they offer the church—are rooted in that rural Protestant ethos I mentioned earlier.

Thus, a second massive revelation has to do with the diminution of full leadership within a religious institution because of the clergy's own sense of inadequacy or real incompetency in fiscal matters. Most assuredly, one of the primary reasons for the vitality of the church in America as opposed to the subsidized state churches of Europe has been the need for financial support by its constituents. On the other hand, many of the wounds and deficiencies of modern society go unmet because the voluntary religious institutions have not had enough economic savvy to meet those changes. Housing for the poor and the aged has become a governmental concern which could have been met by nonprofit charitable institutions who understood the power of credit as it pertains to their structure. Obviously, one hesitates to suggest simplistic solutions for very complex social problems, but I must declare that a more materialistic clergy, in the sense I am using here, would make a far greater impact upon our society than has been the case to date.

Clergy should take a long, hard look at their paychecks: they reveal much about their self-perceptions and their task of leadership in a voluntary institution.

My second example is that *clergy should work less and have more fun.* Howard Clinebell, Jr., of the School of Theology at Claremont, California, said, "Clergy tend to have a high work addiction, and a low pleasure anxiety." Unfortunately, he is probably right.

In 1934 the working class in America adopted the five-day work week. That work pattern has been normative in America for more than thirty years among most classes and vocations, with the exception of the clergy. Clergy still negotiate contracts with a proviso for one day a week off, and then proceed to violate that provision regularly. The status symbol for clergy is not the size of the paycheck or the size of the church: it is the crowded datebook. How often does this happen? Two ministers enjoy each other's acquaintance and they say, "Let's get together again soon." Out come the datebooks, and they discover their next free night is six months away. That little vignette must happen frequently. It happens often enough for Dr. James Glasse to have given it a name, the "conform/complaint syndrome."[1]

The syndrome Glasse describes applies to a variety of clergy phenomena. Clergy can identify critical factors which influence their work and lives, but they seem unwilling to attack those factors with the intention of changing them. They make an uneasy peace with the pressures upon them, often sighing that such is simply the minister's lot. Thus, it is supposed that the busy minister is the involved, creative, and productive minister.

Balderdash!

In an interview in the September, 1972, issue of *The Christian Ministry* writer and management consultant Peter Drucker points out that in our language we have a word for "activist," meaning "one who is active," but have no word for "accomplishmentist," meaning "one who accomplishes something." As a group, clergy tend to be activists, judging themselves and their performance by that criterion rather than looking at their accomplishments and measuring their expenditure of time and resources in terms of the results they produce.

To be sure, there are some anomalies about the work of the clergy which make their work addiction difficult to alter. Of necessity they work most when others are at leisure: nights, weekends, and holidays. That does seem to "come with their territory" and is not in itself detrimental. But when ministers couple this "leisure worktime" with the compulsion to work a "more normal" five-day work week as well, it is not surprising that they find themselves working sixty to eighty hours a week. Not surprising, but unhealthy and unwise.

A second anomaly is the peculiar leadership status and style of the ministry. Ministers may be the titular heads of a congregation, but usually they stand outside the administrative structure of the institution. They are ex-officio to boards and committees, advisors to the congregation rather than its decision-makers. They have an indirect rather than a direct role in the decision-making process. How often clergy find themselves wishing they could "do it themselves" instead of investing hours in teaching others to do it.

A third anomaly is the vague set of goals with which the clergy seem to be content. They see themselves as enablers, helpers of individuals and groups struggling to cope with the vicissitudes of life. Ministers seem to possess a Messiah complex which expresses itself in the belief that if they just had a little more time they could get everything straightened out.

The work addiction of the clergy produces a collateral phenomenon: an uneasiness with leisure, recreation, and pleasure. The residue of the Puritan ethic hangs over them in theological language. They find their justifications in work not faith. In Transactional Analysis language, their Adult selves take command, inhibiting their Child selves from the freedom to frolic. Even church programming initiated by the clergy tends to be of the consequential type, less frequently of the fun and games type. The increase of leisure pursuits by the society has left the clergy at a loss. They tend to feel threatened by the laity's long weekends, summer cottages, and winter vacations. Steeped in the historical ethos of rural, hard-working American Protestantism, they see such diversions as problems for the maintenance of the institution, not as opportunities for retooling church styles and programs.

There are many tentacles to the work/leisure issue. One of these is right under the minister's nose: his or her family.

The American family lives in changing patterns. Ministers know this from their counseling of others, but their own work addictions and pleasure anxieties sometimes make them insensitive to the changing patterns of their own families.

The changing role of women is affecting many families, and the parsonage family is no exception. Ministers' wives are experiencing new freedoms and opportunities. The placement system has a new component that greatly affects its wheezing machinery— ministers' wives who have good jobs and do not want to move when their husbands do. Denominational officials are now saying that the question used to be "Is there a decent parsonage?" but now the question is "Can they find a position in a brokerage firm for my wife?" Howard Clinebell comments on the demise of the satellite marriage in which the wife's role rotates around that of her husband. Clinebell welcomes a new "equality" in marriage but notes the added necessity of improved channels of communication between husband and wife. Knowing the work addiction factors in clergy, he advises couples to make "dates" in their calendars and keep them inviolate.[2]

Churches seem to be ahead of many clergy in this area. They have reduced their expectations of ministers' wives and have taken the minister's family off the pedestal. Divorce does not carry the stigma it once did.

Ministers' children are also being liberated from the

former patterns of unchildlike behavior. All children today have many more choices about what to do with their free time. The pinch in the minister's house is that the leisure time which society affords many families is work time for the pastor. A year of fifty-two Sundays does not provide many family trips, and a Monday off is not in step with the school system.

In the case of mother as minister still other family adjustments will have to be made. If female clergy find themselves working many hours with little time for leisure, then it is father and children who have to cope in new ways.

None of these changing patterns is unique to ministerial families; all families must come to grips with them. But intentionality in ministers' work and leisure habits is being advocated because unless clergy internalize their priorities they will not respond to changing family patterns. Fathers or mothers too busy to relate to, listen to, and share with their own spouses and progeny cannot be active participants in the changing styles of family living. None of us—least of all clergy—can assume that our families are bastions to which we can repair from the upheavals of the world to lick our wounds. Home is where it's happening, and the clergy—male or female—had better be intentional about their presence and participation there.

A second tentacle of this work/leisure issue has a future consequence with immediate implications. Retirement is a new fact of life for almost all people. Statistics show that we can expect to live longer. We have more choices to plan for, and new styles of life to learn. That's the rub for work-addicted, leisure-leery persons.

Clergy have had economic problems in their retirement. Many clergy now retired earned a mere pittance in their productive years and receive a percentage of a pittance for life in their golden years. Examples of the gross insensitivity of the church as an employer are rampant when one examines the estates of elderly clergy. Fortunately, some churches are waking up to this outrage and do make efforts to grant supplementary incomes to pensioned clergy.

Two policies prevailing in some pension boards ought to be challenged by clergy because they reflect a professional paternalism toward the recipients of pensions. First, individual clergy ought to decide when they should retire and begin drawing benefits. The Bismarckian sixty-five is not sacred. Some clergy ought to retire earlier and some later, but in any case the clergy and not the directors of the pension board ought to say when their time has come. (Incidentally, I have a hunch that some problems of the alleged clergy surplus might be resolved by earlier retirement options. Some clergy might retire early, draw a small pension, and serve a small church which is not "economically viable." The current crunch of excess clergy is *not* in small parishes; it is in the larger churches. The choice of an earlier retirement just might start a natural selection process which would realign clergy in churches.)

The second pension board policy that should be challenged has to do with a lump payment at the time of retirement. Some clergy cannot afford to retire, because they have lived for most of their professional life in a parsonage provided by the church. When the time comes for them to retire they are shocked at the cost of buying a home. Surely, the option of taking a portion of one's retirement resources for home ownership would enable some clergy to manage life better in their older years. (Another, to me, sensible advocacy is to urge pension boards to invest some of their extensive holdings in long-term, low-interest loans to agencies that would build, own, and manage housing specifically designed for retired clergy.)

To be sure, either of the above advocacies would mean that clergy would have less dollars than if they retired at sixty-five and took regular monthly payments. The key word is *options* for clergy; let the recipient make his choice. Further, it should be noted that these are, at best, remedial steps. They are suggestions for coping with clergy economics as they have been and are, not as they ought to be in the future.

But the substantive issue as regards older clergy is not economic; it is personal. Ministers who earlier in life had work addictions and pleasure anxieties are ill prepared for a retirement of fishing and golfing. One or two intentions must be incorporated into one's life beforehand. If one must simply sigh and say, "God help me; I am a workaholic," then one's retirement must have an activism in it. Clergy should begin at an early age to learn that second vocation or that hobby that can become a semi-vocation in retirement. Or, and this would be my preference, before retirement one becomes intentionally at ease with leisure. One begins to understand that God's gifts include both work to do and time not to do work.

Denominational judicatories, if they were not staffed by work-addicted bureaucrats, could be helpful. A built-in program of R and R (rest and recreation) could be a part of their mission and ministry to clergy and their families. The Puritan past makes such ideas draw sneers, but I suggest that a block of symphony concert tickets for clergy and spouses might bring realistic awareness of what there is to enjoy in a world of work.

I think clergy should work less and play more. Such an advocacy is directed at external conditions, but its force and necessity are directed at the inner person. Specifically, I argue that the small issue of work/leisure is the result of the absence of intentionality about who one is and what one does.

In this context intentionality begins with self-appraisal. What, from among the minister's many skills, do I do best and most enjoy doing? Once again, the rural Protestant past makes this difficult because one parson and one church are expected to offer a full range of religious services. Specializing in your particular area of competency may be difficult, but it is not impossible. It is not impossible for two very valuable and little-celebrated reasons: the elasticity of the church and the freedom of the ministerial profession. Churches are pliable; they do bend, and more often than not they do not snap when bent. That is one good reason for mobility among the clergy. Churches may find renewal for a time under good preaching alone, but then they need a supplementary emphasis upon small groups or religious education or social action. But time after time I have been amazed at the way churches respond to a minister's emphasis on his specialty and survive the mediocrity of other areas. The clergy who strive to be all things to all segments of the congregation are depriving themselves of one of the great joys of the ministerial profession, the inordinate freedom to shape their work according to their skills, interests, and competency.

A necessary second component of this intentional process is to share one's own intentions with the congregation. Clergy are irresponsible about teaching the laity who they are and what they can do. In the absence of this teaching about the profession, great aberrations develop. Many myths about what it is like to be a minister persist among congregations because clergy do not choose to dispel those myths. The sad consequence is that lay expectations of a particular minister are shaped by the memories of other ministers they have know.

The inauguration of a new pastorate is the ideal time to set forth one's intentions in this ministry. If you prefer to be called at the church during working hours rather than at home in the evening, for God's sake say so! Just because your predecessor did not object to some pattern this does not mean that you must follow in his way. The truth is that the congregation expects you to be different, but it is up to you to say in what ways you are different.

After self-appraisal and teaching others about their work, the clergy must embark upon a rigorous and systematic pursuit of these intentions. It is in the execution of these intentions that the notion of intentionality comes apart. It does so because clergy are bombarded with opportunities to serve. With their high degree of commitment they find it difficult if not impossible to say no. The inevitable conclusion is that their energies are dissipated, they work sixty to eighty hours a week, and their special talents are underutilized.

One of the reasons it is difficult to execute one's intentions in ministry is that there is little evaluation of clergy vis-à-vis their own announced intentions. The enormous freedom to shape one's professional pursuits can be a curse if one is not called upon to account for the use of that freedom. Further, if a minister has not set forth his intentions he will be evaluated on the old, cumulative expectations that the laity have acquired from years of preacher watching. Thus, a fourth step of evaluation is necessary. If one's intentions were to work fifty hours a week and take Tuesdays off, then one ought to be asked why one failed to do so.

Finally, then, the massive revelation attendant on this smaller issue of work/leisure is that clergy lack a focus, a special purpose, of their own choosing for the enrichment of their work. Lacking that focus, they tend to dissipate their resources and are judged by irrelevant standards of achievement.

One of Parkinson's laws was that work expands to fill the time allotted to it. This law applies to the ministerial profession. If clergy do not shape their work and their working conditions, their work and their working conditions will be shaped for them. Only through intentionality and negotiation with others about those intentions will there be any real change.

A third small issue which yields massive revelations is that *clergy should be defining what success means for them and their work.* "Success" is often a "no-no" word among clergy; they think of themselves as being above the rat race, keeping up with the Joneses, selling their souls for some temporal gain. I certainly hope that they are above or away from that nonsense. Nevertheless, they are human beings. As such, they come with ego needs, the necessity for satisfactions and fulfillment. They have symbols which represent the external gratifications of these internal needs. I plead here for clergy to put forth some candor about their human needs and declare for themselves just what success means to them.

Since the term "success" has been preempted by our commercial society and its mundane connotations are unacceptable to clergy, there are certain other euphemisms which will do. "Achievements" or "accomplishments" might be more acceptable terms. Quite simply, clergy need some handles for knowing how they are doing. Are they getting anywhere? Are they progressing toward some objective, or drifting toward an unknown rendezvous?

One of the smaller, hidden revelations to be seen in this issue is the complications which result from our lack of some agreed-upon definition of success. The most dramatic evidence of this negative effect is "the moving syndrome." The Council for Church and Ministry of the United Church of Christ reports that the typical pastorate is of slightly more than three years' duration. Someone should calculate in dollars and cents what this frenetic moving costs the church—and the clergy. The restlessness of the clergy, would I think, prove to be an expensive habit. More important, I believe that the moving syndrome among clergy is used as a substitute for success. That is, one thinks one is making progress because one makes a change. Most denominational structures offer so little in the way of job enrichment that they encourage clergy to repeat the same patterns in differing locations. As Jim Glasse puts it, "If a clergyman says he has had fifteen years' experience, the changes are that he has not had fifteen years' experience at all—he has had three years' experience five times over!"

The ministerial profession itself suffers penalties in the absence of a definition of success for the profession. Consider these questions and the tentative answers given to them: Who says who and what a minister is? Under what conditions shall he or she provide his or her services? How shall he or she be educated to begin and continue his or her education throughout? How does he or she know he or she is growing and improving in the practice of his or her profession? Those are the success questions which all clergy have and must answer. Lamentably, my observation is that they are being answered—but by others, not by the clergy. Consider the ways in which the following four entities answer those questions for the ministerial profession.

1. The Seminary. It is hard to imagine a skilled minister who is not grateful to his or her seminary for the preparation for ministry he or she has received from a school of higher education. But a seminary is just that—a school of higher education. It takes many of its models for excellence and success from the academic world. Students are given grades as symbols of their success. They write papers and meet the criteria academia has provided, for certification to the church and the world that they are educationally fit for the ministry. Given that learning experience—and added to all the previous years of education it represents nearly the sum total of the young minister's life and a fourth of the mature minister's life—it is not surprising that clergy see themselves, in part, as mini-professors. Their models are academicians, not pastors. Their skills are academic, not pastoral. Fortunately, if they have been well educated they begin to make the transition from dependent students to independent professionals, but, alas, too often the weaning is traumatic. The point is that clergy carry with them a model of successful ministry which has roots in the academic world. What do you do when the congregation does not ask you to submit a paper at the end of the quarter?

2. *The Laity.* According to the Internal Revenue Service clergy are self-employed, and that is true up to a point. But in ways direct and indirect, the clergy are supervised and called to account by the laity. Although it is glossed over and decorated with picturesque terms, the fact of the matter is that parish ministers work for a lay congregation, and the laity use certain indices as measurements of success.

The criticism I make here is not so much that the clergy work for the laity as that the laity are too easy on the clergy. Most people hold an opposite view, which is expressed most frequently in the notion, "You can't please everybody." Nonsense! The laity let the clergy off where they ought to be pushed, and push them where they ought to be let alone. Frankly, laypersons, except for a delightful few, do not have the imagination to envision the possibilities of the ministry, and they do not have the experience to know its limitations. Clergy do, but they are reluctant to share that knowledge with the laity or, worse, with each other.

Thus, lay congregations fill in the answers to the success questions for the clergy, but their answers lack a creative awareness of ministerial possibilities. The really sad consequence is that clergy know what a lay congregation expects and tend to shape themselves to those expectations.

3. *The Denomination.* Local churches belong to a denominational system. This belonging has varying degrees of reality and effectiveness for clergy. But for the most part denominations retain control over the placement system, and that mightily affects the clergy. The self-interests of parish ministers are not identical with the self-interests of the denominational system. It would be gross incompetency for a denominational official to place a hostile critic of the denomination in one of its most influential churches.

The denominational system functions largely because clergy and local churches "own" the aims and objects of the whole denomination. But the owning process is, shall we say, enhanced by the placement power that resides within the denomination. To overstate the case, there are punishments and rewards which the denomination can confer upon churches and clergy. Knowing that, it is in the clergy's own interest to conform to the expectations of the denomination. In that way the denomination influences the answers to the questions of success. Clergy are organized vertically in denominations rather than horizontally in peer groups, so clergy take their clues more from the denomination than from each other.

4. *The Culture.* Everybody knows what a minister is. They have seen Billy Graham on television, have read Norman Vincent Peale, or have seen Bing Crosby in *Going My Way.* Clergy are easy stereotypes. Never swear around them. Kid them if it rains on your picnic. Be surprised if they divorce. The culture has a whole set of expectations about what ministers are and do.

There was no more dramatic example of this than in

the civil rights struggle of the sixties. The culture expected clergy to stay in their pulpits, not march in the streets. Because the culture had missed Niebuhr and Bonhoeffer, it was not prepared for an active ethical expression of faith.

It is my observation that clergy are uncomfortable with the stereotypes of the culture, often to the point of being embarrassed to say what they do for a living when meeting strangers in a neutral setting—like the first tee of a golf course. The hesitancy of the clergy in those moments is not so much shame at their profession as the recognition that the stranger has a stereotyped image of who and what a minister does. The culture has told him.

These, then, are four possible sources for expectations surrounding the ministerial profession. The seminary, the laity, the denomination, and the culture all contribute to the standards of ministerial excellence, achievement, accomplishment, career development, or success.

The massive revelation in the smaller issue of defining success, then, is that the clergy themselves have little to say about the ways in which these questions are answered. The four groups who do give answers have a disproportionate voice, not by design or even intention, but by default. The clergy have let other people usurp the self-determinative powers which are rightfully theirs.

Even if you buy this analysis there are no simple, easy solutions. Clergy tend to be loners, they have a barely concealed rivalry with their fellow practitioners, they have adapted to the system and have little heart for changing it.

Nevertheless, I am so bold as to advocate the creation of professional associations for clergy. I believe the fault lies not with the system but with the clergy themselves. They will get what they deserve, especially other people's answers to the questions about success in their profession. If they cannot answer those questions for themselves then they deserve to have to live with others' answers.

Salary, work/leisure, and success are not big issues. They are not causes which summon persons to battle or call them to new heights of creativity. But in and through these smaller issues are revealed some substantive matters affecting the vitality of the church and its missionary purposes.

Stated negatively, these three smaller issues suggest the price of being unintentional about ministry. If clergy fail to be intentional about themselves and their purposes, the intentionalities of others, by default, will become theirs.

Or, to put it more positively, as one becomes more intentional about who one is and what one does, the possibilities for self-direction and peer accountability become far greater. I cherish no vision of a ministerial profession which is arrogantly self-assertive, or conceived for self-perpetuating purposes. But I do long for an aware clergy recognizing that their own unintentional conduct does not liberate or enrich them.

Throughout this essay I have used the word "professional" without attaching a particular definition to it. To be sure, there are many definitions of the term which help advance its understanding, but one that I find particularly helpful is this: a professional is one who does what he does with self-critical reflection about himself and his performance. Too much of contemporary ministry is visceral response to external stimuli.

I write to call my colleagues in ministry to a conscious self-criticism about issues small and large, to the end that we may liberate and direct the best that is in us to the service of Christ and his church.

NOTES

1. James D. Glasse, *Putting It Together in the Parish* (Nashville: Abingdon Press, 1972), pp. 19-20.

2. Charlotte H. Clinebell and Howard J. Clinebell, Jr., *The Intimate Marriage* (New York: Harper & Row, 1970), p. 59.

Part V

INTENTION AND CONTENTION: SOCIAL ISSUES IN MINISTRY

Negotiation in ministry takes different forms in a changing culture. Negotiating an intentional ministry is a helpful model for facilitating and responding to those changes. The first two chapters in this section describe how blacks and women in ministry challenge the accustomed ways of the church. The third chapter describes helpful strategies for negotiation and intentionality in contemporary social change.

Black Ministry

CORNISH R. ROGERS

Despite the fact that black church life and white church life have been separated for a long time in this country, there have been significant instances of confluence between black and white clergymen throughout their joint history in America. There have not always been segregated Sabbaths. Blacks and whites often worshiped together in the North during the 1800s, and occasionally black preachers were called to white congregations. In fact, black colonial preachers practiced their ministry almost entirely before white or interracial congregations.

Black preachers, slave and free, received their theological education from white missionaries or Bible schools, of course. It is clear that black preachers patterned their vocational image after white preachers. But when it became obvious that, on the whole, white congregations and preachers did not accept blacks on an equal basis in the churches, blacks withdrew to themselves and, following the lead of the slave preachers, restyled their churches and ministry to serve their peculiar circumstance. Free blacks in the North and the South had to develop churches which not only reaffirmed their worth as a people but which also institutionalized whatever meager power they possessed

Cornish R. Rogers is associate editor of Christian Century and pastor of St. Paul's United Methodist Church, Oxnard, California.

collectively to protect themselves from social injustice. Black slave preachers had to develop a language and style which made coherent the broken past, the alienating present, and the hopeful future of their black slave congregations.

In the process of dealing with the existential situation of the people they served, therefore, black ministers had to plumb deeper into their own reservoirs of creativity to fashion a vocational style quite different at points from the white style they were taught. A change in vocational self-image occurred simultaneously. Call it African or Afro-American, the new image took on distinctive features which have evolved through the years to characterize the black minister. Black preaching tends to be more evocative and descriptive than didactic. Its message always stresses the awfulness of the present followed by the glory of the future. The black church operates its interior life as a family. Indeed, there is evidence that the black church preceded the black family and became, to some extent, its prototype. After manumission, black churches sprang up rapidly in the South to provide social organization for familyless ex-slaves. The black preacher became a father figure—invested with power—and not a suffering servant figure, as many white ministers are expected to be. Moreover, the black preacher was looked upon as a leader to be followed rather than a model to be emulated. He was for his charges God's holy priest; the Protestant notion of the priesthood of all believers was not sociologically or psychologically applicable. He was also a power broker between the black community and the white structures of power.

But most important, the black preacher served as an indispensable cultural linkage figure. During the relentless wave of black migration from the South, he alone represented the link with "home." He created familiar space for rural blacks who found it difficult to feel at home in an alien urban setting. Since he was probably born in the South as most members of his congregation were (until recently), he reminded them of the old home values they were tempted to discard and helped to domesticate the strange environment into which they had been thrust. In short, he provided continuity and stability for his people—in much the same way that white foreign-language preachers aided the European immigrants at the turn of the century.

Because black preachers tended to relate more to congregations than to hierarchical structures, they found it necessary very early to learn the delicate art of negotiation with congregations for their pastoral services. It is no coincidence that the overwhelming majority of black preachers are Baptists. It is also no coincidence that black preachers tend to display that skill most desired by congregations, preaching ability, although this is changing. Hierarchical sending structures are more concerned with polity faithfulness and administrative skills on the part of the preacher, but as congregational power of ministerial selection increases—and there is evidence that it has—the process of negotiation will become more commonplace even within hierarchical church bodies.

But the average black preacher still differs from most white preachers in at least two important respects: his entry into the ministry probably stems from an avocational choice rather than a vocational one; and he is usually prepared to earn his living in another occupation if he cannot negotiate a satisfactory contract with a congregation.

With the exception of a few hierarchical black church bodies, notably Methodist, the black preacher is unencumbered by strict qualifications of education and ordination. Therefore he does not have to make a decision early in his adult life to become a preacher. He may have been trained as a schoolteacher, postal worker, or life insurance salesman. His interest in the ministry may have been nurtured by his participation in church life as a deacon or other officer in his local congregation. Asked by his pastor to carry out some part-time sacerdotal duties, he may have been ordained by him and employed as a part-time minister of education or visitation, while at the same time working full-time at a secular job. Then, as he acquires additional skills by observing the pastor and by getting opportunities to preach at minor services and on other occasions, he may decide to offer himself to another congregation, or a schismatic faction within it, as a preacher candidate. He will then be in a position to determine whether it will be more feasible to remain at his secular job or to accept a congregation's offer. If he decides to accept a congregation's call, he will probably quit his secular job after a short testing period; or he may continue his secular work if his congregation cannot provide full-time remuneration. When he has developed the congregation enough to receive full-time support, he may drop his secular job.

Very seldom does a congregation expect the minister's wife to be included in the contract, although many wives do take traditional "Mrs. Reverend" roles seriously and work alongside their husbands in the church. Moreover, some wives are public figures in their own right, and often pursue professions of their own. The image of black ministerial leadership, however, is clearly not that of a "parsonage family," but of the preacher alone. Negotiations are therefore made exclusively with him, and his abilities are of primary interest to the congregation. Some black churches have been known to look the other way when their favorite preachers were beset with marital problems or married again.

Since black preachers are on the whole not considered father confessors, but community leaders, they are not called on to provide much personal or marital counseling. One does not ordinarily go to a community leader of high social standing with one's personal secrets. This is in stark contrast with the average white minister, who is often deluged with the counseling needs of his congregation.

The kind of black minister just described does not often come into substantive contact with white clergy, but he strongly influences the style and shape of ministry of his black mainline denominational clergy neighbors, who do relate to the white church world. By example and through competition for souls, he reminds other black clergy that their congregations respond to certain intonations, gestures, and emotional cues which they must provide in their preaching if they want to fully satisfy their hearers. He also serves as a model of autonomy. He comes and goes according to his own schedule, not the church's. Often much of the priestly and pastoral work of his parish is performed by assistants, both lay and clerical. His congregation apparently understand clearly that he is not expected to do their bidding except for a delimited range of duties mutually agreed upon. In most instances, he must only preach, pray, and keep the church afloat financially. His freedom of ministry in the black community often evokes envy among his colleagues in mainline denominations, who, though they feel superior to him in many ways, look upon him with grudging admiration for successfully pursuing an intentional ministry.

Black ministers feel a special need to negotiate an intentional ministry because they and their congregations know that the minister must be free if he is to be a successful power broker for the black community. His congregation must understand that his daily schedule should be flexible enough to permit him to deal with extraordinary contingencies often related to the civil rights or social welfare of his community. He is, literally, expected to *be* the church in the community, and, as such, must not be *bound by* the church. Above all, he is the official proclaimer of the gospel—the gospel of freedom. And if he is not free, he cannot secure freedom for them.

Freedom is, in fact, the cardinal theme of the normative black church. As titular leader, the black preacher is expected to demonstrate by example what it means to be free. For the ex-slave, freedom meant several things. First of all, it meant the opportunity to come and go at will, without having to ask permission of a higher-up. After manumission many freedmen flocked to the roads and later along the railroad beds, sometimes traveling to and fro aimlessly, as if to "try out" their freedom. Secondly, freedom connoted the right to consummate legal contracts, such as marriage. Jewish pushcart salesmen in the South are reported to have had a run on cheap wedding rings immediately after the Civil War as freedmen strove to legitimize previously informal sexual relationships. Education was highly regarded by the ex-slave as a major concomitant of freedom. To be able to read and write was considered irrefutable proof that one was free. Finally, the show of wealth, indicating financial self-sufficiency, was also included among the major effects of freedom. The black preacher is expected by his congregation and the black community to be the embodiment of those effects. His congregation therefore understands his frequent out-of-town trips and does not expect him to keep regular office hours. He is expected to dress well, and the congregation often assists him to do so, to some limited extent, with gifts of clothing, furnishings, and occasionally a new car. In many instances the preacher is the most educated person in the congregation, and if he is not, he is considered, at least, the most self-educated person, often speaking with an orator's affected accent. Many black preachers who missed the opportunity for extended formal education find a way nevertheless to "earn" a "Doctor of Divinity" degree from a local Bible College or by mail from a correspondence school of questionable credentials. The walls of most black preachers' studies, or dens in their homes, are studded with "degrees" or certificates of legitimacy.

What is important, therefore, is not the substance alone, but the "appearance" of possessing the effects of freedom. It is of crucial importance to understand that the normative black church is concerned about the "feeling of liberation" as well as its substance. Because of continuing oppression of blacks in various subtle forms, black congregations want preachers who will at least help them "feel free." Like the Roman Catholic priesthood, which holds the power of salvation through the sacraments, the black preacher is the only one (save alcohol and drugs) who can deliver the feeling of freedom to the black Christian churchgoer, and no price is too high to pay for him. And like their slave forebears, black church members still want the experience of having their "spirits float free" though still about their hands they "feel the chains."

Because of what he stands for and what he can deliver of that "needful, hurtful thing called freedom," the black preacher is well armed to negotiate an intentional ministry.

Women in Ministry

BURNICE FJELLMAN

What are we to say to and about women ministers? Does all that has been said elsewhere in this volume apply equally to women in ministry? The answer must necessarily be ambiguous.

In general, *yes,* women in parish ministries have the same basic training and apprentice experience which ideally prepare ministers for effective service. They too need to be intentional about the vision of their ministry for the years they serve; they need to negotiate the living-out of that vision in their professional careers. Goal-setting and evaluation are important for professional women, also, as are the dominant reference groups (the congregation, the denomination, and peers). The "small issues" (compensation, the work/leisure tension, the meaning of success and retirement) have relevance for them as well.

On the other hand, *no,* what is said does not apply equally to women ministers.

In the first place, there are few women in parish ministries. It is difficult to get an accurate figure concerning the number of women who are ordained or serving congregations, but it would be a small percentage of the total number of ordained ministers.

Burnice Fjellman is associate executive of Professional Church Leadership for the National Council of Churches.

However, the increasing number of women in theological schools (the American Association of Theological Schools reported that in the fall of 1972 women represented 10.2 percent of the total enrollment in the seminaries) means that we can anticipate more women entering parish ministries (if they succeed in getting placed).

A second factor has to do with the denominations themselves. There are still major denominations which do not ordain women. In those which have ordained women for many years, there is still the matter of placement; these denominations have women awaiting calls to congregations. In the denominations which have voted in recent years to ordain women, there are few women who have been ordained and fewer who serve as parish pastors.

Finally, while the sexist language in this volume has been kept to a minimum, the content has been written by males (except this brief statement) and reflects their experience and thought patterns. All of which is to say that women ministers who read this volume will do so critically and warily.

However, a book such as this cannot avoid taking into account (though briefly) women ministers, with particular reference to where they come from and the forces which influence or motivate them. There are consequently a number of assertions which can be made concerning women in ministry.

1. Women come to parish ministries with the required training and apprentice experience, *but* culture, socialization, and tradition affect the way they appropriate this training and experience and translate them into practice.

Any woman who declares herself for the ordained ministry knows she will meet resistance from individuals (women as well as men) and from institutions. Some women (perhaps more in the older age group) have had to use an inordinate amount of persistence just to get an undergraduate degree, let alone any kind of graduate education. It is accepted, for example, that male children will attend college, but since females are destined for marriage and family roles, attending college is an elective which can be denied or made difficult. Such experiences leave their mark, and for a woman to suggest that she aspires to the ordained ministry intensifies the struggle.

Women have been limited in their roles by tradition and by a culture which says they are homemakers, teachers, nurses, social workers; they are nurturant, passive, men's servants and helpers; they are not equipped to participate fully in the church's work; they lack achievement drive; and they are fulfilled through men while men are fulfilled through their work. Such role stereotyping has been accepted by women as well as men, and resistance has thus had to be faced on two fronts. This socialization process has a detrimental effect on both sexes. Both have been denied the right to express themselves in other than stereotypical ways in work, word, and actions.

In "Who Become Clergymen?" (*Journal of Religion and Health,* January, 1971) Jack Bloom discusses the "marks of the clergy." He focuses on pulpit clergy and pulpit seminarians as he looks for common personality correlates that apply to most groups of clergy. In studying results from the Minnesota Multiphasic Personality Inventory (the personality inventory most widely used with theological students) he indicates some *suggestive leads* (he is careful not to draw conclusions), namely, sensitivity to others, the need to succor and nurture, and the dependency-passivity syndrome. These will be recognized as characteristics which culture labels as feminine. Further on in the article, Mr. Bloom draws on other studies to indicate that the desire to love and be loved is a strong characteristic of these men, that they have a deep inner need to help. Again, these are usually labeled feminine qualities.

Other characteristics noted in the same article are a sense of differentness and set-apartness, which may give us a clue to the resistance of men ministers to women ministers: what the men have considered to be their turf is being challenged.

Depending on individual experiences, women entering parish ministries are aware of these forces. Not a few will be jolted into a new awareness of them as they negotiate their roles in parishes. Clarity of purpose (mission) is therefore essential for women in parish ministries, because they cannot take for granted acceptance of themselves in this role by their congregations or their peers. They are going against the grain, so to speak, and must determine how best to maintain their integrity as they seek to win the support of some, if not all, who resist.

2. Women *have* demonstrated intentionality in overcoming the obstacles to becoming parish ministers.

Collectively and individually, women have persisted in their determination that God calls them, also, to the ordained ministry. In recent years the women's movement has had its impact on the churches, especially manifested in the task forces, caucuses, and committees which are challenging the churches on issues related to women in church and society. These groups have done research, have presented resolutions, and have prodded denominational governing boards to make policy and procedure changes which enhance the role of women in the church. They have demonstrated a kind of group intentionality to bring about changes in their particular denomination and in so doing have strengthened the resolve of their sisters in other denominations. Where once the lone woman had to decide whether to risk her future by asking for ordination or to be content where she was, she can now count on support from many women within and outside her denomination.

The individual woman minister must still, however, demonstrate her own intentionality. Intentionality for women is closely related to motivation and achievement factors which have been controlled through the socialization process. Femininity and achievement are both desirable traits, says society, but they are mutually exclusive with respect to occupational choices. If women have any achievement motivation, it is toward marriage (says tradition), while men are motivated toward education and work. For a married woman to seek fulfillment outside the home and family is subtly questioned, and the single woman is looked on "with suspicion and horror." The more successful a woman becomes, the more society fears she has lost her femininity, but a man becomes more attractive as a husband and father.

Women making career decisions and opting for the ordained ministry are not only making a choice among professions, but must deal with conflicts between the roles expected of clergy and the roles expected of females in relation to the family. Single women feel these same pressures, since all women have been conditioned from early childhood to behave in family-role patterns.

3. Women have considerable experience in negotiating which is not readily accepted by the church as a valid part of their preparation for ministry.

The church as a voluntary association is stressed elsewhere in this book. Much of what is said about the church as a voluntary association can be said of women's auxiliaries and organizations, which are also voluntary associations.

The history of most women's auxiliary organizations in the church reveals that they were begun because women were denied full participation in the affairs of the church. Because women felt a sense of mission and wanted to share in proclaiming the gospel, they negotiated a place for themselves related to, but independent of, the official structures, where they could plan and implement programs and projects, elect officers, develop their own budgets, and raise the money to meet them. These auxiliaries have been tolerated—and ridiculed—by the dominant male members, who have never hesitated to accept money from them. The church has benefited greatly from the effective educational programs sponsored by women's auxiliaries. Lay women are probably better informed about their denominations and the church generally than most lay men.

Women's auxiliaries were also in the forefront of ecumenical and interdenominational cooperation. Some women's auxiliaries have given up their lives in the hope that the time had come for a fully integrated church where women could be equal participants in all the church's affairs. This goal has not been accomplished, and many women are frustrated by the vacuum which has been created. A number of denominations still have strong women's auxiliaries, though these are probably more closely interwoven with the church structures than the original organizations. In either case, caucuses and task forces have come into being to raise the consciousness of the church concerning the role of women in church and society.

The legacy of these auxiliary organizations is a corps of women trained and experienced to be intentional and to negotiate among themselves and with church officials with whom they have sought to be partners in mission. The churches, by and large, have not been willing to acknowledge this experience as valid preparation for ministry.

Women have also been part of other voluntary associations, e.g., the YWCA, parent teacher associations, Church Women United, the League of Women Voters. Each of these has provided an opportunity to develop and sharpen the skills which women can bring to ministry and other leadership roles in the church.

These various organizations and auxiliaries have shared another characteristic, namely, a collaborative style of working and supporting each other in achieving a common goal.

Women—married or single—have also negotiated the time and space for a personal life, which has meant giving attention to homely details, such as shopping, meals, laundry, cleaning, entertaining, and other social amenities. Single professional women do not have "wives" who assume these responsibilities, and married professional women usually do double duty.

In addition, there are women who have developed skills through experience in "secular" occupations and professions which should be considered assets if and when they wish to enter professionally into the life of the church. The church, however, finds it difficult to accept any of these experiences as valid preparation for ministry.

4. If we "develop models for behavior by observing patterns of behavior in others" (Biersdorf), it is stating the obvious to say that women have lacked female models for ministry and that observing the male model is inadequate.

The lack of female models in ministry is a factor in motivation or intentionality. With few models in congregations, few women classmates in seminary, and perhaps not even one female faculty member, the young woman aspiring to the ordained ministry has been influenced almost entirely by male behavior patterns. Even history has been written in such a way as to obscure the role women have played in church and society. Among the publications which seek to fill this gap is *The Lady Was a Bishop* by Joan Morris (New York: The Macmillan Co., 1973), which is the hidden history of women with clerical ordination and the jurisdiction of bishops. It is a well-researched and -documented book which illuminates a neglected aspect of ecclesiastical history.

If a woman comes to terms with society's criticism that a female is unsuited for the ministry, she still has no model except the male minister. If she evidences too many of the so-called male characteristics (e.g., aggressiveness, creativity), she will be criticized by women as well as men. If she tries to be her own person, her female counterparts as well as fellow classmates may accuse her of romantic rather than priestly motivations. In short, she has no assurance that she will be accepted seriously as a woman minister. She is always under pressure to prove herself in a way no man is expected to do.

Women are more and more insisting on the right to their own style of living and leadership—shaping their careers to meet the needs of people and society from where they are experientially and theologically.

If there are to be female models for future parish ministers, women must be supported in their exploration of a variety of ways to respond to the needs of people. Internships and field work must be defined so as to maximize the possibility for this to happen.

Ways must be found to draw together the experiences of women theological students in order that the women may strengthen and support each other—and discover models now lacking. Such a process should include a study of team ministries, with special reference to male-female teams. Particular attention should be given to what happens when additional members join an established ministry, usually headed by a man.

5. Placement and mobility are critical factors for women in ministry. A large proportion of ordained women have been placed in small parishes (often rural), or they have become assistant pastors, directors, or ministers of education. There is a lack of mobility for women in ministry from small to larger parishes, from assistant or associate pastor to head or chief pastor, from clerical to administrative to executive positions in the church hierarchy.

A lively and provocative discussion was carried on by thirty-four women and men present at a Consultation on Women in Ministry in December, 1973. Recognizing the absence of women in professional positions in the church and the increase of women preparing for ministry, the following needs were noted:

a. A personnel service which would provide a flow of information among denominations on women seeking employment in the church
b. A service which can provide guides and models for the placement of men and women in the church
c. A strategy within the denominations to force the existing structures to work for women rather than set up a counterstructure

Women are challenging the hierarchical structure of the churches and the systems employed by them. Meaningful changes will be accomplished only when men and women determine that they will be a "counterforce to all that demeans a person" (Sister M. Thomas Aquinas Carroll, RSM, *The Experience of Women Religious in Ministry of the Church* [Chicago: National Federation of Priests Council, 1974]).

6. Women in ministry will increasingly challenge the

male image of ministry which is perpetuated in the written and spoken word, in architecture and forms of worship.

The very presence of a woman at the altar or in the pulpit will be a reminder to worshipers that references to God have traditionally been in male terms only, that masculine nouns and pronouns are consistently used in the creeds and hymns, that women are missing in decision-making positions in the church. No longer can church members be allowed the luxury of closing their eyes to these inequities. Women ministers will challenge the "cop-out" that "man" is a generic term and that "everyone" understands that it includes women too! They will call attention to the fact that denominational publications perpetuate the male image in their educational materials, official statements, church papers, etc. They will help the people in the pew to realize that even when neutral language is used, they may still have a mental image of men in leadership positions in the church. They will conduct Bible studies in such a way as to remove the blocks to a deeper and truer perception of Jesus' message concerning women. "In him the so-called feminine qualities of compassion, care (the hen gathering her chicks), self-sacrifice, love, tears, passiveness before the Spirit, longing for unity, reconciliation and forgiveness *prevail at least as much* as his so-called masculine traits of initiative, confrontation, courage, aggressive condemnation of enemies, leadership, independence of judgment. No wonder that Julian of Norwich could write: So Jesus Christ who sets good against evil is our real Mother, God is really our Mother as he is our Father" (Carroll, *The Experience of Women Religious* . . . , italics mine).

READ ON!

BIBLIOGRAPHY

The following selected titles are a good place to continue the discussion of women in ministry—to *hear* what women themselves are saying and feeling about their call to ministry.

Beyond God the Father: Toward a Philosophy of Women's Liberation. By Mary Daly. Boston: Beacon Press, 1973. A scholarly attempt to explore the ramifications of sexism for women. A basic presupposition of the book is that sexism is ontological.

Our Call. Frances Todd, ed. Wayne, N.J.: Sheba Press, 1973. Sixteen Episcopal women share their thoughts, feelings, and experiences as they have responded to the call to the ordained ministry. As the editor states, "they reach into their inmost roots to find the substance for reaching out and risking themselves in exposing for your eyes the struggles they have known and the Grace they have received in hearing their call and in responding."

Sexist Religion and Women in the Church: No More Silence! Alice Hageman, ed. New York: Association Press, 1974. Paperback. This book grew out of the experience of the Women's Caucus at the Harvard Divinity School. Funds were secured from the Lentz Lecture Fund for a series on women and religion in 1972–73. The volume contains the lectures and one of the significant and provocative papers written for the seminar on "Women and Religion in Sexist Society." Some of the titles: "Preaching the Word," "Women and Ministry," "Black Women and the Churches: Triple Jeopardy," "Judeo-Christian Influences on Female Sexuality," and a view from the back of the synagogue—"Women in Judaism."

Women: A Selected Bibliography. Patricia O'Connor, coordinator. Springfield, Ohio: Wittenberg University, 1973. Paperback. This bibliography was part of a two-year project, Woman and the Human Revolution, funded by the Lutheran Church in America to explore the proper response of educational institutions to current questions concerning the nature and role of women. The principle of selection employed was to include a sampling of classic works, some period pieces, and current research.

"Women in Theological Education: Past, Present and Future." Emily Hewitt, guest ed. *Theological Education,* vol. VIII, no. 4 (Summer,

1972). American Association of Theological Schools, P.O. Box 396, Vandalia, Ohio 45377. A series of essays by ten women and one man, discussing out of personal experience the role of women in theological education. The editor states, "If women want a role in theological education, we will have to claim it. This issue of *Theological Education* is about that claim."

Women's Liberation and the Church. Sarah Bentley Doely, ed. New York: Association Press, 1970. Paperback. This book represents a pioneering effort to portray the new demand by women for meaningful participation in the church, to ground it theologically, and to gauge its impact on the future of the church.

"Women Theologizing." *Christianity and Crisis,* vol. 34, no. 1 (February 4, 1974), pp. 1-16. In the opening essay, Sarah Bentley Doely and Claire Randall discuss "The Spirit Moving: A New Approach to Theologizing." Women have learned that theological reflection is best done in community; our theology expresses a communal experience, reflects the fact that sin can be societal, and provides support for members. The essay is followed by a three-part drama, written by the ten women who were members of the Work Group on Myths and Images at the 1973 Grailville Conference on Women and Theology. The third item is an essay by Phyllis Trible, "Good Tidings of Great Joy: Biblical Faith Without SEXISM."

Strategies for Social Change in the Seventies

SPEED B. LEAS

THE INTENTIONAL PASTOR

In his book, *To Come Alive!* Jim Anderson tells the story of a mythical pastor and his relationship with his flock:

> We live in a culture in which the suppression of differences by those in power—parent, superior, teacher, social class, or nation—has been a strong influence on our choice of conflict management style.
>
> Take, for example, Pastor Smith, who was greatly concerned about a "conflict" he was experiencing. A small group in the congregation seemed to him to be opposed to everything he wanted. The budget, which he felt had been amply reviewed in the finance committee, was hotly contested at the following meeting of the congregational board. The pastor's every emotion was to rid himself of the conflict. He was not able, even with help, to be skillful in understanding what was happening or to stay in touch with the impact of his own behavior on the other people involved. His personally unacceptable anger at being opposed was expressed as cold withdrawal and hurt feelings. In the stress of the conflict the pastor reverted to old and unproductive ways of responding to those who differed with him. The result was that some of the "opposition" left the

Speed B. Leas is director of training for the Institute for Advanced Pastoral Studies, Bloomfield Hills, Michigan.

congregation and others simply became quiet. The minister then began to express his concern over the dull, drab, lifeless apathy of the board meetings.[1]

This, says Anderson, is illustrative of a more general stance among clergy: they are "seeking to remove the distress caused by conflict rather than looking for help to accomplish positive goals." This situation in which the pastor finds himself highly invested in and deeply affected by the subject at issue, is like those in which he finds himself committed to social goals which are either not understood or are resisted by the rest of the congregation of which he is a part. Because of this resistance, feelings of anger, frustration, resignation, or impotence have a more profound impact on the pastor than does the mission to which he or she is committed. These feelings have a strong effect because they are experienced as existentially real, while the mission, the task, and/or the necessary process for accomplishing this task come to be perceived as distant and removed from the press of relationships, possible disappointments, fears of being regarded as ineffective or inadequate, or not being admired.[2]

We must deal with our feelings appropriately if we are going to be able to manage and develop a significant social change ministry. I was struck recently by the way the pilot of an airplane in which I was flying handled an aircraft malfunction, loss of the hydraulic system. The fuel had to be jettisoned, the landing gears cranked down by hand, and an emergency landing made at the nearest airport. Had the pilot been extremely frightened by this situation he could have lost control of the plane and/or he could have generated panic and terror among the passengers. But his communications from the cockpit were to the effect that this was routine, it was no big deal, there were emergency systems to back up the ones that had failed, we should all have a drink and sit back and relax, and, by the way, "sorry for the inconvenience." Because the pilot had confidence about what he should do in this situation, because he knew what to do with the plane and what to do with the passengers, and because he was able to manage his feelings, not only was he able to control the plane, but his behavior helped the passengers "control" or manage their feelings of fear and helplessness.

Leaders in the sensitivity movement have held as one of their fundamental theses that people were not aware of their feelings and should (indeed must) get in touch with them. The implication was that we were able to suppress or avoid our feelings and, hence, not deal with them. This led to loss of energy, displaced aggression, emotional explosions, and denial of what was happening. It seems to me that the perceived problem was poorly stated. Pastors, lay leaders, members of congregations, judicatory officials, and so on have always been in touch with their feelings. They have always been super-conscious of their fears, their joys, their needs. The problem has been one of inappropriate, ineffective, or counterproductive mechanisms for coping with these feelings and the situations which generate them, as was the case for Pastor Smith.

This is what is at the heart of the "problems" related to the effective implementation of social change ministries in the church. Instead of being able to cope with (to implement change in) social ministries, church persons have spent their energy seeking to remove the distress caused by differences of opinion, resistance, and change, rather than developing and maintaining strategies for accomplishing positive goals. Committing one's energy and resources merely to removing stress means that one will feel guilty and unhappy about having accomplished very little and quite likely one will have made the situation worse.

In order to be able to implement social change ministries an integrated process which deals both with feelings and with change strategies must be implemented. An intentional ministry committed to social change will have the following four characteristics: (1) the pastor will have an internalized theological knowledge and commitment; (2) the pastor will know how to show the congregation the functional relationship between the faith of the church and the issues under discussion; (3) the pastor will know how to show the congregation processes and behaviors which will help them cope with the feelings which arise and the decisions which must be made; (4) the pastor will value, work for, and sustain supportive interpersonal relationships.

Theological Knowledge

The educational experience of many pastors has led them to learn what *others* know rather than to become aware of and articulate about what *they* know. One's seminary experience and the processes by which one is evaluated often focus upon rehearsing a list of the five arguments for the existence of God or what differentiates Barth from Brunner. When pastors see theology in this second-hand way, they distance themselves form their own experience and from the experience for which the persons in the congregation are looking.

John Fletcher of Inter/Met says that this kind of behavior moves the authentication for the pastor's and layperson's work to externalized sources (the seminary, scholars, or the denomination). Fletcher says that "the real process of being confirmed or authenticated as a spiritual leader will come only in the mysterious intersections of his own spiritual biography with hundreds of other lives. Every event in the parish, every meeting, every liturgy, is an opportunity for spiritual growth and leadership."[3] Fletcher describes the externalized authentication experienced by members of the congregation which he found in a study of laity he did in preparation for the development of the Inter/Met experiment. Small groups of laypersons were asked to describe the five greatest problems they had experienced with clergy. The same responses occurred again and again: the "first intensely felt problem was always what one layman called 'religious inauthenticity,' others described by terms like 'pious and hypocritical,' 'he speaks down,' 'he doesn't have his head and his heart together.'" These are the results of ministers' external authentication and knowledge. Not only are they unable to move others to commitment and action because the themselves are perceived to be uncertain, though they won't admit it (hence, the description hypocritical), they are also unable to follow through on their own quasi-commitments because these are not fully internalized and owned.[4]

In a social change ministry the sources of authenticity and internalization of knowledge are regularly revealed within the walls of the parish and without. In the sixties and early seventies, those of us who were working in the civil rights movement and against white racism were constantly tested by the minorities with whom we were working. The greatest concern was that we would be a "white liberal"—a term which to me means one who has not internalized his or her commitments and knowledge. White liberals said they were for integration of the races, but were paternalistic in their dealings; when asked by blacks about their commitment, they would avow loyalty to the movement, but when given an opportunity to be counted they would sit silently.[5]

Internalized theological knowledge means that one clearly knows what one is committed to, and the extent to which one is committed, and one is able to state one's position authentically because one is motivated by the need to state the position, not the need to protect oneself or to blame others. Thus it is possible to describe one's position, state why this position is held, and not feel compelled to blame, shame, or condemn others with divergent points of view.

Showing the Relationship
Between Faith and Social Action

The link between one's faith and action is crucial for the Christian; if this link is weak, he or she will be criticized as being either all talk and no action or all action with no foundation in knowledge or faith. The intentional pastor knows why he or she is in action and is able to articulate the meaning of that action in terms of his or her religious experience. The intentional pastor also knows how to use himself or herself in the social action process and can choose among various change strategies. Persons in the Action Training Movement have often noted that it is not possible to get church members to "think themselves into new ways of acting." They have cited the number of times they have led Bible study groups, preached from the pulpit, shown exciting and dramatic films, and led people through the reading of the latest and most provocative best seller calling for social revolution or reform; and each "event" is met with a need for further discussion and a resistance to action. These people are like those who have taken many music appreciation courses in college, have read the history of the development of music, and have taken courses on music theory and harmony; they may have even taken a course on the construction of musical instruments, so they know how and why each makes its own unique sound. Nevertheless, without learning the skill of coordinating hand, eye, and ear, one cannot play any instrument.

On the other hand, one who is all technique—has only learned to play by practice and does not understand harmony, or what Bach intended a particular piece of music to mean, will not be able to express himself or herself with anything more than pedestrian banality. So, in the church, there are those individuals who are busily engaged in social change, never being quite sure for what purpose. When they are challenged about the meaning of their actions, their answers are weak and do little to inspire others, or are unclear and do little to maintain commitment when the going gets difficult.

Having observed a good many ministries, my perception is that our style of life in the church in the United States is such that we have erred on the side of too much theory and not enough practice. We don't know how to analyze community needs, we don't know how to organize people, we don't know how to run effective meetings, and—most important of all—we don't know how to use ourselves as effective agents for change within the church. Because of this awkwardness in the realm of behavior (as opposed to thought) we are unable to involve others effectively in change processes. Linking ideas and action is impossible when one of these is underdeveloped. Intentionality requires the development of the skills of change agentry and the ability to show the functional relationship between what one thinks and believes and what one practices and does.[6] It is important to be intentional not only about what to do, but also about how to do it.

Helping Others to Cope with Feelings

In addition to knowing what to do and how to do it, the intentional pastor must know how to deal with his or her own feelings and help others manage theirs. Our culture has taught us that unpleasant feelings are signs of failure and that the causes of those feelings should be avoided. However, as one begins to study situations in which "negative" feelings arise, one begins to discover that these situations are the times when individuals are learning, growing, and developing.[7] Anxiety, stress, and tension are the normal and healthy concomitants of change, whether that change be for good or evil. Indeed, the fact that we are anxious about any change means that before the change is implemented we will examine it, to the extent possible, and test and review it, to be as certain as possible that we are indeed making a change for the better and not for the worse.[8] In order for a group to make an effective and intelligent decision, then, there needs to be a certain amount of anxiety so that all ideas are carefully reviewed and tested to determine their viability before their implementation. The problem comes when we assume that, since I am anxious or someone else is anxious, our energies should be used to remove the anxiety. Removing the anxiety means either that the ideas do not get challenged or that no change is possible because it raises anxiety.

The intentional minister is one who understands the dynamics of anxiety in groups and helps the group cope with its anxiety by doing the following four things.

1. The pastor sees anxiety and potential conflict as an occasion for growth. Questioning leads to clarification of the various alternatives, as we have indicated above. But more than that, as individuals question proposals for change they get a better understanding of them; they become less threatened as they understand more, and they develop less opposition and (often) more commitment to the proposal. Initial resistance is often the healthy reticence of persons not wishing to commit themselves to something they genuinely fear might be

foolish. Reactions of frustration and anxiety to this initial resistance may lead to increased resistance and anxiety on the part of the questioners. Nondefensive, factual presentation and sensitive listening to the questioners can reduce anxiety and increase persons' commitment to and participation in the proposal being suggested. Thus, what was originally perceived as conflict can become the occasion for clarification, commitment, and growth as persons learn to deal with their anxiety nondefensively.

2. The pastor tells the truth. I used to be very confused when non-church people would tell me they didn't go to church because Christians were hypocrites. Sure, I knew of some instances of Christians who had "gone astray," but, by and large, my experience with church people was that they were a relatively moral, straight bunch of people. Recently, I have come to realize that the hypocrisy people described was less that related to so-called mortal sins and more that related to an area of behavior which I used to think was petty, but which I now see as fundamental to my full life as a person. The so-called pettiness consists in telling ourselves how much we love one another, when we are stiff, formal, and uncomfortable in one another's presence; it is expressing dissatisfaction with the pastor in the parking lot or on the telephone but never in a church meeting or to his or her face; it is naming our shortcomings in the prayer of confession but never at any other occasion in our life together. Denial of our frailty, uncertainty, and inadequacy has made us hypocrites to ourselves and to others, and this denial keeps sabotaging our attempts to gain others' trust and commitment.

3. The pastor begins where people are. In their zeal to prove that they are competent and effective in the ministry pastors often hope for more than is possible and push people beyond their limits of toleration. This

pushing has obvious consequences for the pastor's effectiveness, but it also affects the way pastors feel about themselves. Pastors who expect more than is possible from their congregations are frustrated and dejected. Those who begin where people are and then expect more each year from their congregations are continually challenged by their work, are excited by its new possibilities (they don't get bored with the same old routines and programs), are having regular small victories in which they can take pride, and are aware of their growth and development as leaders.

4. The pastor seeks to integrate diversities. How often have you heard it said of a pastor that he or she is a great pulpiteer but awkward with people face to face. Or, this pastor is a wonderful counselor but can hardly manage himself or herself in the pulpit. Pastors do not have the luxury of being good at one thing to the exclusion of competence in others. They must be able to integrate theory and practice, their inner life and their outer behavior, their ability to give to and receive from God and other people, their own personal growth and service to others, meetings their own family and personal needs and helping the church fulfill its mission. None of these poles contains the fullness of life; it is in the dialogue between them and their integration that one begins to sense the fullness of intentional ministry.

Commitment to Relationship

Jay Hall, in a conflict management inventory that he developed for management,[9] has clearly shown that there are two excessive styles of conflict management. One is the excess of commitment to one's goals, to the exclusion of caring relationships with others. The minister with this style loses sight of his or her role as pastor and becomes "fixated" in the role of prophet. He or she tends to ride roughshod over the feelings of others and pushes his or her point of view without regard for what happens to persons in the process, unless concern for persons is clearly necessary to achieving the goal. On the other hand there are those who see relationship as being the highest good and have such a commitment to maintaining warm, close, personal relationships that they lose sight of the mission and purpose for which the church is called together; indeed, sometimes they assume that the only mission of the church is to maintain warm, close, personal relationships. With such exclusive commitment to relationships, commitment to ideas, standards, and goals get lost in the fear that our good feelings might be lost and the church might become a chaotic den of bad feelings. So other commitments are set aside to maintain "the fellowship."

Getting locked into either of these extremes means that little happens that the people of the church find fulfilling. And it means that the pastor has lost his or her commitment either to persons or to the mission of the church. The key to intentional effectiveness is not to "temper" (which usually means to moderate or mitigate) one's commitment either to goals or to relationship but to hold each commitment passionately. This means that we not only care deeply about what we are doing but also care about our life together. Intentional ministers know what they believe, they are able to state it clearly and succinctly, *and* they are able to listen with concern, openness, and interest to what others have to say— showing that they care about them and what they have to say. Commitment to other persons does not mean that I must agree with what they say or what they do, but it does mean that I am supportive of them and that I keep working at developing our relationship, rather than avoiding or attacking the other person, or concentrating on defending myself. I know who I am and what I am about and thus do not have to break the relationship in order to know who I am.

SOCIAL CHANGE STRATEGIES

As I pointed out earlier in this chapter, it is not enough for pastors to want to be involved in social change ministry. In addition to the commitment, they must also have skills and knowledge. The second half of this chapter will deal with four strategies[10] which pastors might use to involve their congregations in such ministries.

Helping Strategies

The first method for social change that is often used by persons in the church consists of what I call helping strategies. In helping strategy, one becomes aware of a need that another person or group has and then mobilizes the resources available to meet that need. The helper may be aware that a certain family is going through hard times financially and can give that family some money from a discretionary fund. Or a church may become aware of the fact that there are many mothers who need to work during the day, and it may seek to help them by getting the government to fund a day care center to be housed in the church. This list of helping strategies could go on and on: hot lunches for senior citizens, drug counseling centers, Christmas toys collected for the poverty community, etc.

There are several problems associated with helping ministries, however. Indeed, the problems with helping ministries are so severe that there is good reason, in most cases, for trying to avoid them entirely. This is not to say that in some situations helping strategies are not necessary and appropriate. But in the long run they tend not to produce what is needed and to lead to dependency and difficulty rather than health and interdependence.

The first problem with helping strategies is that they tend to lead to dependency on the part of the recipients.[11] Whether one is talking about giving "answers" to theological questions, or giving food to a destitute family, the "answer" or food may be absolutely necessary on a short-term survival basis, but unless people are able to develop their own theological competence or financial base, they will be caught over and over again without skills and resources to take care of themselves.

Not only is dependence a problem, but also (and this is the other side of the coin) dependency means that there must be a patron or organization who is the care-taker, the "daddy," the benefactor, the supporter, the helper. Patrons make people feel like children, and patrons make themselves feel superior to others. In the patron-dependent relationship, there are few options for growth and development. The dependent persons tend to feel that the only options open to them are obsequious subservience or rebellion. An intentional ministry should be one in which the social change strategy intends the independence, at least, if not the interdependence of the group or individual being served. The only kind of helping that can do this is the kind which has built into the very roots of the relationship (1) the intention to make persons responsible for their own lives, (2) the intention to develop systems which will foster and enhance individual and group independence, and (3) the measuring of success by behavioral rather than sentimental standards. The "payoff" for many engaged in helping ministries is the warm feelings they get from "doing for" others. Indeed, if the standard of success that one establishes for oneself is that the relationship feels warm and pleasant, one can expect the endeavor to be doomed to failure in the long run. The intentional minister whose criterion for success is individual and group competence in coping, knows that much of the growing that must take place has at the root of its processes feelings of pain, frustration, and agony that come from the risky business of being independent.

Are there times when helping ministries are appropriate? My answer to this is "hardly ever." Any ministry whose goal is to help others is doomed to being a part of an agenda of pacification and subjection. From time to time an emergency will arise where the situation calls for an exception to the rule. Families flooded out by a rampaging river, one spouse and the children deserted by the breadwinner, a drug-dependent teen-ager who does not know how to cope with life any longer asking to be put in a place where he or she will not have access to drugs—these situations demand a response which puts the victim in a dependent position. The point is that one must recognize the deleterious effects of the helping and develop a strategy for moving beyond it in order to release the victim from the bondage of catastrophe.

Educational Strategies

The next three strategies, educational, contest, and collaboration, are those which I would recommend as having the greatest possibility for use as social change strategies in the church. None of these strategies enjoys the luxury of avoiding contention or pain in the church. They are selected, not because they will cause less trouble (either in the sense of being a bother or in the sense of surfacing unpleasant feelings), but because they will move the church in the direction of accomplishing the social goal intended. We in the church usually tend to believe that somehow good feelings are necessary for institutional survival. In fact, the ability to cope with bad feelings is what is really necessary for institutional survival. It is not possible to sustain the warm glow of fellowship 365 days per year. A healthy church is one in which, when "trouble" arises, healthy people are able to cope with the difficulty, understand it, and develop strategies to deal with the relevant issues. Those who must avoid and repress uncomfortable situations are only setting themselves up for an ineffective, untested, uninteresting, monotonous life.[12] A counselor does not design his or her therapy to help people feel good all the time. Indeed, an effective counselor helps persons cope with bad feelings, and coping doesn't mean making them go away forever. The counselor recognizes bad feelings as indicators that a person is at a place where new growth and development can take place.[13] The same is true for the local church. The time of pain indicates that the church now has the potential for growth and strengthening. Times of pain are times of opportunity. Pain avoided is an opportunity lost. Pain dealt with may mean the loss of some members who are not ready for growth, but it may also mean a stronger and more competent organization.

An educational social change strategy assumes that the major change target is the ignorance of the persons who can effect the change. For instance, if one wishes to work toward the elimination of the white racist practices and policies of a local church, one cannot assume that the members of the congregation recognize or agree with the idea that they are white racists. In order for them to come to this understanding, it may be necessary to take them through a number of educational experiences, which may include reading books, holding discussion groups, engaging in exposure experiences, seeing films, listening to sermons, going on tours of certain sections of the city, passing resolutions, and so on. The purpose of these experiences is to help the members of the congregation to become educated about the effects of their current policies and practices.

The role of the pastor, when using this kind of strategy, is usually that of an educator or teacher or persuader, though sometimes the pastor may function as an administrator—recruiting the leadership for the training sessions and facilitating the smooth implementation of the educational plan.

In choosing an educational strategy, there are two things that the effective persuader will want to watch out for. The first and foremost concern is that in his or her educational zeal a dedicated persuader may have a tendency to move from education to deception. That is, when the educator is trying to persuade another of what he or she believes is right, there is a tendency to forget to tell the whole story and to tell just those things that will be favorable to the educational goal. For example, the dedicated anti-white-racist, in seeking to make a case for more sympathetic understanding of the plight of black folk, may deny the horrendous problems of the welfare system or may present a naïve picture of welfare fraud.

Another problem that sometimes arises with regard to an educational change strategy is that the "study" group just keeps on studying and never finds a way to move from concern about issues to being actually engaged in developing and implementing a change strategy.

Contest Strategies

Another social change strategy that is often used in the church and is the essence of our governmental system in the United States is contest. In this method the pastor, organizer, or group leader tries to mobilize the amount of power necessary to "win." In different organizations under differing circumstances power takes varying forms. Sometimes power is embodied in an office or individual. In The United Methodist Church, for example, the bishop has the power to install pastors in the pulpits in his conference, and also to remove them. So, if we wanted to influence clergy placement, we would work on the bishop. In other settings, power means getting a majority vote. So, in Congress, if we want to pass a certain bill, we must garner 51 percent of the votes cast. Sometimes power is lodged in persons who are influential, though not in authority. This is usually what is meant when someone is described as a "pillar of the church." A "pillar" doesn't necessarily have the power to make authoritative decisions as a bishop does, but he or she may greatly influence or affect the voting of the rest of the group. "Unless Mr. Brown goes along with the decision, we'll never get it by the board," represents the kind of thinking I am referring to here.

Voting is the contest strategy most often used in the church. Sometimes contest strategies are overt, as when a group in the church seeks to get friends to attend a meeting; sometimes they are covert, as when a group "surreptitiously" has certain persons nominated for offices in the church so as to be empowered to shape decisions in the organization's life. In some social change contest strategies, the church uses the courts to influence certain social policies or practices, as the United Church of Christ did when it took certain Southern radio stations to court for programming which, in their opinion, was not in the public interest. Martin Luther King's Southern Christian Leadership Conference often used contest strategies for social change. Sit-ins and boycotts are win-lose strategies seeking to achieve ends that are perceived to be worthwhile.

There are four problems in using contest strategies. In the first place, when a leader decides to enter a contest to achieve certain ends he or she must recognize that the contest strategy will result in the opposition's becoming organized almost to the same extent as the "home team." In the civil rights movement this was called backlash. To the extent that persons were organized to protest segregationist policies and practices those who felt that segregation should be maintained were also awakened and enlivened.

In the second place, one must be aware of the very strong tendency in the midst of a contest to escalate from dealing with specific issues to generalizing and personalizing the struggle. It is very difficult for persons in a contest to see the opposition as human beings engaged in a struggle because it is something they believe in rather than from "impurity" of motive. In a contest we begin to see our opponents as incarnations of evil rather than persons who happen to have a different point of view. Moreover, there is a tendency to move from the specific to the general. While the battle may begin over the right of a certain government to govern a certain piece of territory, the battle takes on larger proportions very quickly. It isn't just a piece of land we are fighting for, it is Truth, Justice, and the American Way. Fighting for generalized issues makes it most difficult to remain rational and keep the weaponry from escalating out of control.

Third, in a contest there is a tendency for the combatants to lose sight of why they got into the battle in the first place, and to become more committed to winning than to improving the situation they are in. This is part of what happened when Richard Nixon took the U.S. troops out of Vietnam. There were some who, though they had been against U.S. involvement, felt let down that Nixon had been the one (through Kissinger) who seemed to have been able to stop overt U.S. involvement. They would have been happier if their anti-war "teams" had been recognized as the force which stopped overt U.S. involvement.

Finally, there is a tendency in a contest mode to

remain stuck in a contest mode. Instead of clearing up the battlefield after the skirmish, there is a tendency for the combatants to move to new areas of disagreement, even when combative strategies are neither appropriate nor necessary.

All this is to say that contest strategies can be very costly, and can easily escalate out of control and drive the losers from the organization. If we choose to use these kinds of strategies, we should recognize, first, that we might lose and, second, that the costs of the contest may not have been worth the gains achieved through it.

Collaboration

Perhaps the most difficult of all the social change strategies, but the strategy which will achieve the most significant changes, is collaboration. By collaboration, I mean those strategies in which every party engaged in the work is there out of clear self-interest and sees the possibility of getting his or her needs met without depriving the others of the opportunity to meet their needs. When one collaborates, one assumes that a common definition of the problem can be found and that all the various persons and groups that are affected by the problem can achieve some of their goals. Collaboration is not possible in all cases. To assume that all can get their needs met in all situations is unrealistic and naïve. There are many occasions when contest strategies are the only available option because the goals of the various groups are mutually exclusive. It is not possible to elect two persons to the same political office; one must win and the other lose. It is not possible to paint a room two colors at the same time in the same place. The wall must be either red or green. If another (compromise) color is chosen, no one's needs are met. In these cases there must be a winner and a loser.

However, more often than one might at first suspect, there are numerous opportunities for collaborative social change strategies. To assume that we must be in contest will always preclude collaboration. To assume that there is a way to collaborate is the best place to begin. If it is not possible to collaborate, we can then move to a contest strategy. But, when one begins with contest, it is virtually impossible to move to collaboration for it will be too difficult to generate the necessary trust and openness.

An example of a collaborative strategy for social change with regard to equal employment opportunity in a government organization comes to mind. I was asked to help an agency of the federal government to install an affirmative action program, that is, to employ members of minority groups at all levels in the organization in proportion to the population at large. We could have chosen an educational strategy by which we would have tried to show the current employees (and especially the personnel office) what the proper attitude toward minorities should be and would then have tried to show them how to recruit, train, and hire these minorities. We chose not to use such a strategy. Instead, we assumed that almost every person in the organization would be amenable to the goal of integration, and that, if they participated in the development of a plan for its implementation, they would see that their own jobs were protected and they could find ways to recruit, train, and hire minorities at a pace which was equal to that of the "top down" method, and, more important, would not be resisted by those who would be affected by the change. The strategy worked. It was not painless. There was great initial resistance and mistrust. Throughout the process many very painful decisions had to be made. However, after steady and persistent planning, we were able to get an affirmative action plan agreed upon and installed.

What problems does one encounter when using this method? The first is that in a collaborative system there is a predilection to consensus, and agreement becomes more important than change. That is, if we assume that our major strategy for change will be collaboration, we may work so hard at finding consensus that we lose sight of our original intention to achieve change. There was great danger in using collaborative strategies in the equal employment opportunity program mentioned above, because the whites in power might have settled for inadequate goals so as not to alienate or anger the current employees. This difficulty is especially present in churches where the dominant norms penalize persons who challenge the group and press for change. What I am emphasizing here is that collaboration does not mean that ideas go unchallenged and hard questions aren't squarely faced. Indeed, collaborative strategies are probably more difficult in this regard than are contest strategies, because it is necessary to keep the group together and work for a win-win situation, while radically challenging and testing all ideas that come before it.

The other problem in using collaborative strategies is that there is a tendency to exclude dissenters and cover up differences. Because there is movement toward premature agreement, the group will often make "deviants" feel uncomfortable at its meetings and will seek to smooth over, avoid, or repress challenges and differences that get raised.

CONCLUSION

In this chapter I have attempted to make the case for a special relationship between social change and the intentionality of the pastor. That relationship affirms the pastor's competence in theological knowledge, awareness of self, and awareness of strategies available for effective social change ministry. Weakness on any of these "fronts" will threaten the overall effectiveness of the pastor as change agent and as leader of the church.

Our ministry is a part of a whole life which is an organic unity including intentions, behaviors, organized patterns of interaction. In order to cope with ourselves and our organizations we must take each front seriously so that we obtain the best information possible about what to do, get the most feedback possible on how we are doing, and continue to practice (in the sense of improving our skills) in order to improve our competence. The keys lie in these areas: information, feedback, and practice for our work in the church.

NOTES

1. James D. Anderson, *To Come Alive!* (New York: Harper & Row, 1973), pp. 89-90.

2. For a discussion of research on the effect of anxiety on perception and rationality see Ross Stagner, "The Psychology of Human Conflict," in Elton B. McNeil, ed., *The Nature of Human Conflict* (Englewood Cliffs, N.J.: Prentice-Hall, 1965), pp. 56-57.

3. John Fletcher, "Challenges to the Ministry Today," an address delivered to the U.S. Army Chief of Chaplains Conference, St. Louis, March 25, 1974.

4. See the research done by Chris Argyris described in chaps. 2, 14, and 15 of *Intervention Theory and and Method: A Behavioral Science View* (Reading, Mass.: Addison-Wesley Publishing Co., 1970).

5. See Stokely Carmichael and Charles V. Hamilton, *Black Power* (New York: Random House, 1967), esp. chap. 3.

6. See Ernest Greenwood, "The Practice of Science and the Science of Practice," in Warren Bennis, Kenneth Binne, and Robert Chin, *The Planning of Change* (New York: Holt, Rinehart and Winston, 1961), pp. 73-82.

7. Samuel Klausner, *Why Man Takes Chances* (Garden City, N.Y.: Doubleday & Co., 1968).

8. Richard Walton, *Interpersonal Peacemaking: Confrontations and Third Party Consultation* (Reading, Mass.: Addison-Wesley Publishing Co., 1969), pp. 111-15.

9. Jay Hall, *Conflict Management Survey*, Teleometrics International, 2210 N. Frazier, Conroe, Texas 77301.

10. The last three strategies are developed and expanded in Roland L. Warren, *Truth, Love, and Social Change* (Chicago: Rand McNally & Co., 1971).

11. For an ideological attack on systems which create dependency see Paulo Freire, *Pedagogy of the Oppressed* (New York: The Seabury Press, 1971). Also Ivan Illich, *De-Schooling Society* (New York: Harper & Row, 1971).

12. Walton, *Interpersonal Peacemaking*, pp. 111-15.

13. See James Dittes, *The Church in the Way* (New York: Charles Scribner's Sons, 1967).

PART VI

INTENTIONAL MINISTRY
AS GIFT OF THE SPIRIT

The need for the model of ministry presented in this volume grows out of human experience. The model itself is grounded in biblical faith. In this chapter the biblical and theological sources of negotiating an intentional ministry are described.

Intentional Ministry as Gift of the Spirit

STEPHEN CHARLES MOTT

Negotiation and intentionality as they have been presented in this book are organizing principles. Through negotiation the minister puts order into the range of needs, resources, and priorities which are before him or her. Intentionality is an ordering in the sphere of the basic goals and values of the ministry.

Both these concepts indicate a rational and calculating control of the goals and methods of one's service in the church. For some readers the ancient problem of the relationship of Spirit and order is thus raised. They may feel that reason and human decision are falsely imposed on the free exercise of the gifts of the Holy Spirit. Human works seem to be added to faith, and God's sovereign use of his powers is made subject to the mind and will of men and women. Some may question whether a childlike trust in God and a patient waiting for his working have been abandoned. Why not just let the Spirit do its work? To what degree are we free to order the life of the Spirit?

In response to these important questions, which are made more relevant today by the new movements of

Stephen Charles Mott is assistant professor of Christianity and urban society at Gordon-Conwell Theological Seminary, South Hamilton, Massachusetts.

openness to the Holy Spirit, I will argue that we are obligated by biblical example and teaching to apply reason and order to the powers given by the Spirit of God, and that intentionality and negotiation when used correctly conform well to the New Testament patterning of life in the church.

THE ORDERING BY THE SPIRIT

When the effect of religion is seen primarily as a supplying of powers to the believer or the revelation of private mysteries, God's role in redemption will be perceived as disordering the stability of a *kosmos* in rebellion against him. But God's redeeming role in history is an ordering process as well. The work of Christ, while freeing people from the judgment and national restrictions of the Mosaic law, also fulfills the law: it has continuity with God's past ordering of the life of his people.

In the Old Testament Yahweh is prominent in the liberation from Egypt, a disordering event. But with the same event he imposes a covenant upon the people he has set free. This covenant is a comprehensive ordering of life under God.

God's ordering is seen in that the goal of redemption is the reconciliation of all creation to himself (Col. 1:20). By looking at the ultimate ordering effect of redemption, we can perceive the spiritual nature of the processes of ordering in the present. God's redeeming work is described as the breaking into history of the reign of God, a highly ordering concept; yet his reign is present through his Spirit (Matt. 12:28), which we too often view as an image of freedom and disorder. Intentionality, through setting goals and committing the minister to change, can be an expression of faith and hope in God's work in history.

Even our traditions of worship and our historic faith are an ordering of our experience. We do not rest with the private working of the Spirit in us and our particular group, but we find in the church that provided the context for those experiences also the ordering concepts which sharpen our apprehension of our experience and an understanding of our new role.

Order was taken seriously in the early church. Paul revisited his first converts to organize their churches (Acts 14:23). In I Corinthians, Paul tells how he was forced to confront a group of spiritual enthusiasts in the church in Corinth who set the freedom of their spiritual experiences over against order within and without the church. Paul made it clear to them that God "is not a God of disorder" (I Cor. 14:33). If the church lives spiritually, it will be in order.[1] He concludes his classical discussion of the relation of order and spiritual life with the injunction that all things are to be done "decently [cf. I Cor. 7:35] and in good order" (I Cor. 14:40). Thus in the early church, despite its spontaneous and charismatic character, there are definite regulations of a juridical character pertaining to marriage, support of missionaries, and treatment of grievances.

Paul's conception of order, however, is an order which comes from within the spiritual life of the church rather than one which is imposed from without. The ordering was by the Spirit itself through the interactions of charismatic leaders, including free exhortation and admonition. Included among the gifts of the Spirit are the abilities to be controllers and administrators, but these roles are not offices; there are no duties of an office which are conceived independently from a particular person.[2] (Offices do appear in the latest Pauline writings, but they are still filled by men picked and filled by the Spirit.) The validity of these roles rests on the recognition that they are gifts given by the Spirit.

The Pauline conception of church order is akin to the model of negotiation in ministry. There is not a fixed system of order with spelled-out tasks and objectives. Rather, one's tasks are affirmed by the community's recognition of what the Spirit has empowered the individual to do.

Because Christianity is a historic religion based on a historical revelation, the primary ordering force in the church comes from the past. Campenhausen says of the Pauline church, "The word of God is the basic order." [3] The individual ordinances and regulations had to be in accordance with the original teaching, with what Paul had preached from the beginning (e.g., I Cor. 11:23-26; 14:37-38). For this reason, even in terms of the ordering of our ministerial lives and our role in the church, biblical preaching must be given an intentional priority over professional planning and management, as tender roots have a necessary priority over tender buds. It is the ordering of the word of God which gives our religious experiences and thought their distinctive character and for which reason we are called "Christians" rather than "agapists."

This perspective upon the precedence of the message of God's historical revelation is fully grasped by the concept of intentionality. Intentionality must start with a clear affirmation of the transcendent bases of the ministry which is to be negotiated. The evangelical can find this model of ministry to be one of the best because of this stress on clear-mindedness about our ministerial origins and goals.

Intentionality thus reflects the nature of Christian vocation. If a vocation means "participating in a purpose larger than one's own," Christian vocation means being impelled by the unique conviction that God has called us "to the fellowship of his Son, our Lord Jesus Christ" (I Cor. 1:9). The call to the ministry is a specific expression of the call of the gospel to all people. Intentionality in ministry includes an awareness of the uniqueness of our vocation; we pass on not merely the knowledge of a humane discipline, but much more a sharing of fellowship with the Son of God.

The depth of this vocation frees the minister to make bold and long-range plans rather than having his or her career submerged in the solving of immediate problems. Immersed in one's conviction of God's call to grace, one is released to carry out the specific intentions of one's ministry. This is the vocational image that gives coherence and direction to our professional tasks. And because the call comes to us out of the word of God, we are forced beyond the privatized concerns of our immediate community. For that same word of God also calls us to proclaim its message to all peoples and to carry out social justice in the gates of political decision.

TYPES OF BIBLICAL ORDERING
Equality in Community

Campenhausen demonstrates that in the Pauline churches and elsewhere in primitive Christianity the basis of community coherence was not an order externally imposed; rather, the life of the church develops in the continual interplay of spiritual gifts and ministries.[4] The distribution and functioning of these gifts provide both equality and community. It is indicated in Romans (12:3) and stated later in Ephesians (4:7, 16) that everyone has some such gift. The possessors of the gifts are not to lord it over others. Since it is God who supplies the power, one task cannot be lifted over another (I Cor. 3:7). The basis for equality is that it is the same Spirit which produces each gift (I Cor. 12:4-14).

Historically, the great impetus for voluntarism in Anglo-Saxon culture came from covenantal Puritan

223

structures which were built around this premise of equal access to the Spirit by every member of the community. The perspective of mutual responsibility for the structure of the community was a most influential source of the concept of intentional control and change. Passive acceptance of the traditional patterning of life was to be rejected by the Spirit-guided reason which was available to each Christian. Intentionality in ministry finds both its spiritual and its modern historical roots in these ideas.

The ordering of spiritual power lies not only in the equality of the distribution of the gifts. The Holy Spirit distributes the gifts to produce community. The equality does not decline into an individualism of equal monads, each seeking its own course. The purpose of the distribution is common concern. God has given honor to each part so that the parts of the community body "may have the same concern for each other" (I Cor. 12:25). The purpose of the manifestation of the gift is to confer a benefit upon the community (I Cor. 12:7-10). The possessors are not to refuse to have anything to do with one another (12:21).

Intentionality in ministry, correspondingly, is an affirmation of the significance of the church. Because our life together as Christians is designed by God, we stringently examine ourselves to ensure that we are purposefully acting in accordance with the principles of our Christian commitment. Negotiation in ministry likewise affirms the church as Christian community by demanding a willingness to do the hard work of achieving a consensus on how to carry out our purposes instead of taking the easy road of plowing ahead, doing one's own thing, and rebuffing the common effort. By negotiating his or her own role in the church, the minister is purposefully forcing the community as a whole to be intentional about and to negotiate its own ministry; thus the minister's negotiation is an important aspect of an enabling ministry. The negotiation of his convictions in ministry can be a channel through which the Holy Spirit flows to the rest of the community.

When we see that the Spirit grants its powerful gifts so that there may be equality in community, we are compelled to be responsive to the gifts of the other people in the community. A community depends on each of its members sharing in the vision and experience of purpose and mission that holds the group together. For the community to be Christian it is required that the common vision and tasks come from God. Neither the vision of the community's purpose nor the vision of action is the private property of the pastor. A further assumption for Christian community is the conviction that everyone has the possibility of making some contribution. It is the "whole body," because of the working together of each of its parts, which produces the growth which strengthens it in love (Eph. 4:16).

When these assumptions of Christian community are recognized, the traditional patterns of authority and obedience to authority are abolished. Instead the community supports gifts of leadership because they are recognized as gifts of the Spirit, and the leaders still are bound to live "only the life of humility, of the mutual subordination of every member, of a spontaneity as great in serving as in obeying."[5]

Negotiating one's ministry is a way for a minister to carry out these convictions about community life. It assumes that the minister's contribution is only a part of a total network of interacting gifts. He or she has a role to play, but it is only a part of a much larger whole. Clarity is needed so that all recognize what that role is to be. The pastor thus recognizes the access to the Spirit which the others in the church have; he or she acknowledges that his or her ministry is only a part of the ministry of Christ in which the whole congregation participates by grace. Because they are sharers of gifts of the same Spirit, pastor and people are able to trust one another in negotiating their tasks. They will realize that, in the evaluative feedback from each other about how they have been faithful to their agreed-upon tasks, they may hear the voice of the Spirit.

"Do not neglect the spiritual gift which is in you" (I Tim. 4:14). Because we are to be responsible to all the gifts of the Spirit in the community, we must be responsible for our own spiritual gifts. In fact, the above verse indicates that we have a special responsibility for our own gifts.

The concepts of intentionality and negotiation are helps to the minister in this responsibility to the gifts of the Spirit in him or her. Negotiation requires and encourages the pastor to have a respect for his or her own gifts and natural abilities. By being intentional about his or her ministry, he or she is forced to recognize his or her gifts and so set priorities accordingly. To look at this thought from the other direction, planning one's ministry is a way of taking seriously one's call and gifts. A serious look at ourselves is not always pleasant. We not only see the strengths which call for responsible action. We also see the weaknesses which drive us to a greater dependence upon God and which caution us against a lazy attitude about our tasks. Becoming aware of what our abilities and gifts are and negotiating our tasks can free us from the hampering guilt about saying no to causes and tasks that are apparently Spirit-directed. On the other hand, a lack of self-direction affects not only our own well-being but in some way the well-being of the community which is dependent to a degree upon the functioning of our gifts. That one should make peace with factors in one's ministerial situation which hamper the exercise of one's gifts is not valid ordering of the Spirit.

Reason

An important way in which the spiritual powers were ordered in the church was through the proper use of the Christian's reasoning abilities. This form of ordering the life of the Spirit is quite close to the concept of intentionality.

Campenhausen notes the prominent place that conscious, calm, and objective reflection had in the ordering and organizing of the early church.[6] The high valuation placed upon rational ordering was particularly prominent in the Pauline church: "According to the grace of God which was given to me I have laid a foundation like the wise master builder, but another has built on it. Let each observe how he builds on" (I Cor. 3:10). The Greek word *blepein,* which I have here translated "observe," in this context refers to mental functions.[7] Paul specifies a rational control of one's ministry of the gospel. Günther Bornkamm argues that, despite Paul's negative treatment of reason in the unredeemed person, he allots to reason an extremely important role in the Christian.[8] Paul avoids the hierophantic and apodictic style of revelation-speech which discourages rational reflection upon its content. Rather, he uses the diatribe form of speech, in which the hearer is regarded as a partner in dialogue.

When Paul comes to give advice regarding enthusiastic spiritual expression in the church, he leans heavily upon the necessary ordering by reason. Although they were ordinarily related, for the purposes of the situation Paul places the spiritual gifts of prophecy and speaking in tongues in sharp opposition. He describes prophecy as speaking with the mind, while speaking in tongues is speaking with the spirit, and he gives decided preference to prophecy (I Cor. 14:1-33).[9] The reason is that the word of God must be intelligently proclaimed so as to be understood and so that the Christians may be "mature in thinking" (I Cor. 14:20). In another place where he discusses the proper relationship of the spiritual gifts, Paul begins by appealing to his readers to "think so as to be sensible" (Rom. 12:3).

Paul's conception of "mind" (nous) has similarities to our concept of intentionality. For Paul "mind" is seldom "reason" in the full sense; it is an understanding which determines a person's attitude, not just in considering but also in striving and willing.[10] "Intentionality," as we have been using the word, connotes a close attention to the basic understanding of one's own Christian life and a determination to carry it out in specific directions. It is a rational reflection upon the callings and gifts of God in one's own life and a formulation of the goals which will carry them out. Intentionality gives content and purpose to ministry so that the pastor in his or her negotiations and enabling is more than a process director. It also means that the pastor is rational not only in his or her teaching ministry but in any activity which has to do with ordering the life of the Spirit.

Loving Concern

For Paul reason had to take second place to love as an ordering principle: "Concerning meat offered to idols, we know that we all have knowledge. Knowledge puffs up but love builds up. . . . Watch out lest your liberty become a stumbling block to those who are weak" (I Cor. 8:1, 9). Paul does not reject the rational implications of a knowledge that there are no idols, but he calls for a rationality that has as a high premise concern for the weak. The gnosis with which Paul was dealing on this question of freedom to eat food offered to idols was part of the broader enthusiastic emancipation in the Spirit which characterized his opponents at Corinth. Paul uses the principle of love elsewhere in seeking to order their spiritual effluence. He does not question the genuineness of the violent enthusiasm which his preaching released, but he warns that a more significant demonstration of the spirit is ethical conduct and love.[11] Love is the true organizing force in the community. "Let everything be done in love" (I Cor. 16:14). A concern only for freedom in the Spirit does not build up the fellow Christian and violates the principle of seeking his or her good rather than one's own (I Cor. 10:23-24). One does not just follow freedom in knowledge and in the Spirit by making the Lord's Supper a time of public feasting, because this might put the poor to shame (I Cor. 11:22). Paul separates the gifts which build up and sustain the life of the community and elevates them above those which attract attention and excite the imagination of the immature.[12] Paul is blunt: "The Spirit is manifested to each one in order to benefit" (I Cor. 12:7). Ultimately, it is only love which puts even the most spectacular gifts of the Spirit into a meaningful place (I Cor. 13:1-3). Repeatedly, the principle by which the gifts are ordered in the community as to their desirability and public prominence is whether or not they build up the community (I Cor. 14:3, 4, 6, 12, 26, 31).

The implications of this ordering principle for negotiation in ministry are obvious. Christian negotiation is one which seeks to maximize one's ability to contribute to the community, which includes the needs of one's self; it is never a bargaining of rights which are held independently from the community and its needs.

Mission

Because building up the community in love is central to the purpose of the gifts of the Spirit, it is difficult to separate mission from loving concern, as the latter is biblically understood. Mission had a powerful ordering effect upon Paul. He made abrupt alterations in what his conduct might have been according to spiritual knowledge and freedom if he could have tucked his life away from mission and concern for others. "I have become all things to all of them in order that I might at least save some. I do everything for the sake of the gospel" (I Cor. 9:22-23). Mission puts Paul into a teleological framework for decision-making. He acts according to his perception of what the effects will be on his divine tasks. He refuses to baptize in Corinth lest he be accused of building up his own cultic following (I Cor. 1:14-15). He refuses to cash in on his spiritual right to be sustained by preaching the gospel but instead works for his living "lest we cause a hindrance to the gospel of Christ" (I Cor. 9:12).

Christians with a commitment to Christian mission similar to that of Paul must pay attention to the argument that intentionality and negotiation can make them more productive in the tasks of ministry. Intentionality will lead to a better understanding of their goals and the reasons for them and thus will produce a more pervasive commitment to them. Whatever the task, they will not so readily abandon it because it is more difficult than they had imagined or because it now is less popular than when they began. The process of intentionality and negotiation will help the Christian to identify the issues which are crucial, making him or her more responsible for the formative patterns of mission and concern.

Recognition of Evil

The Pauline teaching of the proper ordering of the powerful gifts of God's Spirit is set in a context of spiritual warfare in which truth is countered by deceit, and the Spirit of God by the spirits of Satan. One purpose of God's giving gifts to the church was that all might reach the maturity in Christ where they are no longer carried here and there by every cunning and scheming teaching that comes along (Eph. 4:14). Rational consideration and order must be applied to the realm of the Spirit because the realm of spirit is not occupied only by the Spirit of God. The spiritual conflict is not between externality and order. Rather, the spirit world itself is divided between the forces of God and the forces of evil so that external categories have to be applied to discern what spiritual power is indeed from God. One must test the spirits (I John 4:1). Paul introduces his major discussion of the ordering of spiritual gifts by distinguishing which acclamation of Christ is actually moved by the Holy Spirit (I Cor. 12:1-3).

Negotiation and intentionality are concepts which operate out of an understanding of the possibility of evil in the context of ministry. Not every impulse or drive which arises in the pastor or in his or her congregation is from God. Discerning what is really the direction of God demands that all who are involved in the ministry of the local church be clear about the real purposes of their Christian service and that they carefully examine which patterns of conduct faithfully carry them out.

The minister is deeply conscious first of all of his or her own proneness to evil. Intentionality involves becoming aware of factors other than the Christian principles and goals which have been determining his or her work.

Intentionality has a future orientation. Just as Paul opposed those in Corinth who could gloss over sinful patterns of life with the enthusiastic claim that the powers of the future had become realized in their present, so intentionality denotes an awareness that to be determined by the events and the pressures of the present is to miss the possibilities in the Kingdom and work of God that surge beyond the definitions of the present.

Negotiation denotes a recognition also of the possibilities of evil in the environment for ministry. This recognition is missed in the low-intentioned "storekeeping" ministry which responds primarily to immediate possibilities presented by its environment. The minister should work with an awareness that the demands of the congregational environment may well conflict with what he or she has perceived as God's intention for his or her ministry. There is an imminent conflict which must be faced and negotiated. The intentional minister will work with campaign as well as consensus models.

On the other hand, since God spreads his voice and gifts across the congregation, there is the constant probability that through negotiation the congregation can help us see matters in our intentionality, or in our ideas of carrying out our intentionality, which arise from us rather than from God. Negotiation is a process of finding God's specific will as it lies somewhere in the tension between reliance on the direction that we have heard individually and the community challenge and enhancement of that vision.

NOTES

1. Hans von Campenhausen, "The Problem of Order in Early Christianity and the Ancient Church," in *Tradition and Life in the Early Church,* ed. Campenhausen (Philadelphia: Fortress Press, 1968), pp. 123-24.

2. Hans von Campenhausen, *Ecclesiastical Authority and Spiritual Power in the Church of the First Three Centuries* (Stanford: Stanford University Press, 1969), p. 64.

3. Campenhausen, "The Problem of Order," p. 128, cf. p. 135.

4. Campenhausen, *Ecclesiastical Authority,* pp. 57, 64, 70, 72.

5. *Ibid.,* p. 69.

6. Campenhausen, "The Problem of Order," p. 126.

7. Walter Bauer, Lexicon⁴, p. 143.

8. Günther Bornkamm, "Faith and Reason in Paul," in *Early Christian Experience,* ed. Bornkamm (London: SCM Press, 1969), pp. 35, 41.

9. *Ibid.,* p. 39.

10. *Ibid.,* p. 43.

11. Campenhausen, *Ecclesiastical Authority,* p. 57.

12. *Ibid.,* p. 60.

INDEX